DEVIL'S ADVOCATES

T0341711

DEVIL'S ADVOCATES is a series of books devoted to exploring the classics of horror cinema. Contributors to the series come from the fields of teaching, academia, journalism and fiction, but all have one thing in common: a passion for the horror film and a desire to share it with the widest possible audience.

'The admirable Devil's Advocates series is not only essential – and fun – reading for the serious horror fan but should be set texts on any genre course.'
Dr Ian Hunter, Professor of Film Studies, De Montfort University, Leicester

'Auteur Publishing's new Devil's Advocates critiques on individual titles... offer bracingly fresh perspectives from passionate writers. The series will perfectly complement the BFI archive volumes.' **Christopher Fowler,** *Independent on Sunday*

'Devil's Advocates has proven itself more than capable of producing impassioned, intelligent analyses of genre cinema... quickly becoming the go-to guys for intelligent, easily digestible film criticism.' *Horror Talk.com*

'Auteur Publishing continue the good work of giving serious critical attention to significant horror films.' *Black Static*

 DevilsAdvocatesbooks

 DevilsAdBooks

ALSO AVAILABLE IN THIS SERIES

Antichrist Amy Simmonds

Black Sunday Martyn Conterio

The Blair Witch Project Peter Turner

Cannibal Holocaust Calum Waddell

Carrie Neil Mitchell

The Company of Wolves James Gracey

The Curse of Frankenstein Marcus K. Harmes

Dead of Night Jez Conolly & David Bates

The Descent James Marriot

Don't Look Now Jessica Gildersleeve

Frenzy Ian Cooper

Halloween Murray Leeder

In the Mouth of Madness Michael Blyth

Ju-on The Grudge Marisa Hayes

Let the Right One In Anne Billson

Macbeth Rebekah Owens

Nosferatu Cristina Massaccesi

Saw Benjamin Poole

The Shining Laura Mee

The Silence of the Lambs Barry Forshaw

Suspiria Alexandra Heller-Nicholas

The Texas Chain Saw Massacre James Rose

The Thing Jez Conolly

Witchfinder General Ian Cooper

FORTHCOMING

Daughters of Darkness Kat Ellinger

The Devils Darren Arnold

House of Usher Evert van Leeuwen

The Fly Emma Westwood

It Follows Joshua Grimm

Psychomania I.Q. Hunter & Jamie Sherry

Scream Steven West

Twin Peaks: Fire Walk With Me Lindsay Hallam

DEVIL'S ADVOCATES

CANDYMAN

JON TOWLSON

Acknowledgments

I would like to thank John Atkinson at Auteur for his unstinting support for this project and his editorial guidance. Michael Blyth at the BFI kindly provided me with the programme notes from a retrospective screening of *Candyman* at the BFI Southbank in May 2016. James Gracey did me the huge honour of reading this book in draft form. Special thanks to Craig and Dawn Clark at Roundabout Entertainment, Burbank, CA for their continued generosity and hospitality. I am grateful to Tony Clarke and Picturehouse cinemas who, in November 2016, invited me to introduce a screening of *Candyman* followed by a Skype Q&A with Bernard Rose. I would like to thank Bernard Rose for his time and for agreeing to be interviewed for this book. Finally, I would like to say thank you to my wife, Joanne Rudling, who has provided support and encouragement throughout.

First published in 2018 by
Auteur, 24 Hartwell Crescent, Leighton Buzzard LU7 1NP
www.auteur.co.uk
Copyright © Auteur 2018

Series design: Nikki Hamlett at Cassels Design
Set by Cassels Design www.casselsdesign.co.uk
Printed and bound by CPI Group (UK) Ltd, Croydon, CR0 4YY

British Library Cataloguing-in-Publication Data
A catalogue record for this book is available from the British Library

ISBN paperback: 978-1-911325-54-3
ISBN ebook: 978-1-911325-55-0

Contents

Synopsis..7

Introduction: *Candyman* and '90s Horror..9

1. 'Sweets to the Sweet': From 'The Forbidden' to *Candyman*....................................17

2. Urban Legends, Urban Myths: Adapting *Candyman*..33

3. *Candyman*: Production and Reception...47

4. *Candyman* and the Return of the Repressed...59

5. Sequels, Spin-offs and Knock-offs...95

Appendix: An interview with Bernard Rose...111

Works Cited..129

SYNOPSIS

Chicago, present day. Helen Lyle (Virginia Madsen), a graduate student researching urban legends, investigates a series of murders in the Cabrini-Green housing projects supposedly committed by a hook-handed killer called the Candyman. Residents of the projects believe the Candyman to be the vengeful spirit of a slave's son who was lynched by a mob in 1890 after falling in love and fathering a child with a white land-owner's daughter. Aided by single mother Anne-Marie McCoy (Vanessa Williams) and a young boy called Jake (DeJuan Guy), Helen traces the Candyman's killings to an empty apartment in Cabrini-Green, and is later attacked in a toilet block by a man with a hook. With Helen's co-operation, the police apprehend the attacker, a local drug dealer (Terrence Riggins) who has adopted the Candyman persona in order to terrorise the residents, and the dealer is charged with the Cabrini-Green murders.

In an underground carpark, Helen is visited by the real Candyman (Tony Todd) and placed in a trance. She awakens to find herself in Anne-Marie's Cabrini-Green apartment soaked in blood. Helen is arrested under suspicion of abducting (and possibly killing) Anne-Marie's baby, Anthony. Later, Helen's friend and co-researcher, Bernadette Walsh (Kasi Lemmons) is murdered by the Candyman in Helen's apartment. Helen is subsequently incarcerated in a mental hospital where her psychiatrist Dr. Burke (Stanley De Santis) attempts to convince Helen that the Candyman is a figment of her own psychotic imagination. Helen invokes the Candyman by saying his name five times. The Candyman kills Dr. Burke, enabling Helen to escape the hospital. Helen returns home only to find her husband Trevor (Xander Berkeley) in the midst of a tryst with one of his students.

Isolated and alone, Helen returns to Cabrini-Green determined to save baby Anthony from the Candyman. She finds Anthony inside a giant bonfire in the Green. As she attempts to rescue the child, residents of the Green light the bonfire. The Candyman is consumed by the flames but Helen manages to save the baby. Severely burned, Helen dies soon afterwards. The residents of Cabrini-Green gather at her funeral to pay tribute. Later, a distraught Trevor invokes Helen in the bathroom mirror. Helen materialises in spirit form and exacts vengeance on her husband.

INTRODUCTION: *CANDYMAN* AND '90s HORROR

The early 1990s was a period of relative stagnation for horror cinema. The genre was undergoing a production hiatus, just as it had in the late 1930s and 1950s. Hollywood was still in thrall to the high concept movie. Small independent distributors, the life blood of horror in the 1970s, had gone to the wall. It became almost impossible for low budget horror films to get screens. Moreover, prejudice against horror by the American ratings board (the MPAA) during the conservative Reagan/Bush era, and the amplification of the Video Recordings Act in Britain following the Hungerford massacre and the killing of Jamie Bulger particularly affected horror, cutting off its markets domestically and abroad. Even European horror production was affected by the tightening of international censorship in the '90s.

However, censorship alone was not to blame for horror's misfortunes. By the late 1980s, the American horror film had become caught in a loop of formulaic repetition. Box office receipts for once profitable franchises like *Friday the 13th*, *A Nightmare on Elm Street* and *Halloween* began to flag due to growing audience disinterest. By the turn of the '90s, the American horror film had, in the words of David Church, 'largely reverted back to niche consumption by its cultish fan base, no longer enjoying the wider audiences it had garnered during the 1970s and 1980s' (2006).

In an era dominated by tired pastiche, *Candyman* (1992) remains one of the most original and finest horror movies. Based on Clive Barker's short story, 'The Forbidden', *Candyman* has been widely acclaimed for its social commentary, as well as for its skilful use of horror tropes and cinematic techniques. Its writer-director Bernard Rose has gone on to a distinguished career in Hollywood which has included further notable work in the genre – *Snuff-Movie* (2005), *SX_Tape* (2013) and *Frankenstein* (2015) – whilst *Candyman* has spawned two sequels – *Candyman: Farewell to the Flesh* (1995) and *Candyman: Day of the Dead* (1999) – and inspired numerous movies evoking urban myths and legends, including the financially successful *Urban Legend* franchise.

As a '90s horror movie *Candyman* has prevailed. As well as receiving positive reviews at the time of its release from Janet Maslin at *The New York Times*, Roger Ebert and *Variety*, amongst others, it continues to win new fans and admirers. Rotten Tomatoes (February 2017) reports that 61% of 42 critics surveyed gave *Candyman* a positive review. IMDb (February 2017) rates *Candyman* at 6.6/10 based on 52,323 users. In 2001, the American Film Institute nominated *Candyman* for the AFI's *100 years… 100 Thrills* (a list of the 'top 100 most exciting, action-packed, suspenseful or frightening movies in American cinema'). In 2007, the TV channel *Bravo* included *Candyman* in its 100 Scariest Movie Moments. In 2009, the horror film website Bloody Disgusting listed *Candyman* in its Top 13 Slashers in Horror Movie History. At the time of writing, *Candyman* is celebrating its 25 year anniversary with a host of tribute screenings in America and Britain, including at Aberdeen University in the UK and at the American Cinematheque's Aero Theater in Santa Monica. As the British Film Institute said of *Candyman* in a 2016 retrospective screening programmed by Michael Blyth, it is 'bone-chilling horror with an acute social-conscience… deeply intelligent and stylistically innovative, without ever forgetting to be absolutely terrifying'.

I first saw *Candyman* at the Odeon, Holloway Road in North London on its UK release in March 1993. At the time it was one of the first horror films to be described as Urban Gothic on account of its gritty real-life Chicago housing projects setting and its appropriation (and interrogation) of urban myth. The circumstances of its release – just after the Rodney King riots in Los Angeles – gave the film real resonance. As Barry Keith Grant has remarked, it was only in the 1990s that race emerged as a major theme in horror, and one of the films at the forefront of this wave of race horror was *Candyman* (2015: 7).

But not only did *Candyman* address issues of racism in modern America, it wove in themes of class and gender that were immediately noticed by reviewers. 'Much is in the way of background,' Kim Newman wrote in *Sight and Sound* (March, 1993), 'including the based-on-fact twinning of the Cabrini-Green ghetto with Helen's condominium, a building erected as public housing but converted to yuppie use, so that Helen's trespass begins even before she ventures out among the disenfranchised.' Even Roger Ebert in his review of the film (October, 1992) placed *Candyman*'s gender politics under scrutiny (pre-echoing many academics) before giving the film his trademark thumbs up: 'What I liked,' Ebert concluded, 'was a horror movie that was scaring me with ideas and gore, rather than just gore.' Indeed, *Candyman* is almost unique in '90s horror cinema in that it plays its socio-political cards upfront even as it deals with the metaphysics of horror – with fear, death and transcendence.

A film such as *Candyman* readily lends itself to socio-political interpretations; it thus becomes tempting for critics to label such a film either 'progressive' or 'reactionary' without due attention to its complexities, ambiguities and the context of its production. Robin Wood posits that modern horror cinema represents an eruption of repression in the form of the 'Other'. Otherness, according to Wood, embodies that which bourgeois ideology cannot recognise or accept but must deal with either by rejecting and if possible annihilating or by assimilating and co-opting into the system. Amongst the list of what our culture deems as Other, Wood includes: children, alternative ideologies, the proletariat, ethnic minorities and women (2003: 63-69). Within its discourse *Candyman* seems to explore ways in which several of these groups become dispossessed, demonised and Other, most notably, of course, ethnic minorities (the Candyman himself) and women (Helen).

In many ways, *Candyman* can be seen as a '90s reaffirmation of Robin Wood's seminal thesis on horror: a *return* of the return of the repressed, if you will. *Candyman* is – as scholar Kirsten Moana Thompson has remarked – 'the return of the repressed as national allegory': the film's hook-handed killer of urban legend embodies a history of racism, miscegenation, lynching and slavery – 'the taboo secrets of America's past and present' (2007: 65).

Some critics, by contrast, have read *Candyman* as a neoconservative text and an example of neoliberal racism. 'Horror texts,' Grant maintains, 'possess great potential for widely divergent readings' (2015: 8), and so it is with *Candyman*. However, as I will illustrate in this short book, the two viewpoints in this case are hardly contradictory. And regardless of reading, *Candyman* remains a work of great cultural significance not just as a socio-political horror but as an evocation of the uncanny.

Although critics have discussed *Candyman* variously in terms of race and social class (Briefel & Ngai, 1996; Hill, 1997; Means Coleman, 2001; Hester-Williams, 2004), gender issues (Kuhn, 2000; Hoeveler, 2007) and social history (Wyrick, 1998), few have acknowledged how *completely* the film appears to follow Robin Wood's original 'return of the repressed' thesis in response, almost, to the glut of reactionary slasher movies that had dominated '80s horror. The main aim of this book, then, is to take *Candyman* back to Wood's Marcusian wellspring argument about the function of horror – that the monster constitutes a return in horrific form of all that society represses and/or oppresses: to look at ways in which *Candyman* represents both a literal and symbolic return of the repressed during the George Bush Sr. era.

Along the way I trace the project through its adaptation from Barker's short story to the finished film; investigate the real-life location of its gritty Cabrini-Green setting; and analyse *Candyman*'s examination (and adoption) of urban myths and legends. The *Candyman* mythos will itself become the subject of later discussion as we see how the character has become imprinted in our culture following the *Candyman* sequels and similar *Candyman*-inspired urban legend movies.

Clive Barker has been described as a fabulist and a metaphysician. Inspired partly by William Blake, his fiction explores alternative, parallel universes: liminal worlds where the everyday intersects with mystic planes. His work hinges on transgression and transcendence. In Barker's own words, 'I write edgy stuff with a lot of weird sexuality and strange political angles' (Green, 1992). In chapter one ('Sweets to the Sweet': From 'The Forbidden' to *Candyman*), I begin by analysing the intersection between Barker's work and that of Rose; surprisingly the two are closely connected, even symbiotic. Rose's UK debut film *Paperhouse* (1988) concerned the fantasy world of a young girl, and his subsequent work has shown a tendency towards transgression and transcendence (*Ivansxtc*, 2000), and repeated returns to social horror. Indeed, Rose was attracted to Barker's 'The Forbidden' because he wanted to 'deal with the social stuff' (McDonagh, 1995: 27). Relocating the action from a Liverpool housing estate to Chicago's notorious Cabrini-Green housing project, Rose extended the story, adding the innocent-person-on-the-run plot twist, and took Barker's conclusion further. But the class subtext, the urban legend and the idea of the myth biting back after attempts are made to debunk it, are all there in Barker's source material. The heroine, Helen Lyle discovers that her normal life is more banal and morally dead than the eternal life-in-myth that the Candyman offers her.

'Urban myths are an unconscious reflection of the fears of an urban population': so says Helen's smug university lecturer husband Trevor early in the film. *Candyman* starts out as Helen's investigation into urban myth; ultimately the film becomes about the nature of urban myth itself. In chapter two (Urban Legends, Urban Myths: Adapting *Candyman*) I look at ways in which *Candyman* offers a discourse on urban myth, and how it utilises actual urban legends such as 'Bloody Mary' (say her name in the mirror and she will appear). Social scientists and folklorists have theorised that such urban legends construct and reinforce the worldview of the group within which they are told, sometimes through an acting out of the legends themselves: a form of 'ostension' (Koven, 1999). In *Candyman*, that worldview speaks of minority oppression and the outward projection of the dispossessed as Other.

Part of the film's remarkable social resonance stems from Rose's decision to set his adaptation in the real-life Chicago public housing project, Cabrini-Green. Built in the post-war period, inhabitants of Cabrini-Green were initially a mix of Italians, Puerto Ricans, Irish and African-Americans, but by 1962 its population was almost entirely black. Flanked by upper-middle class neighbourhoods (such as the one in which Helen and Trevor are resident in the film), Cabrini-Green became a notorious inner-city ghetto long before *Candyman*. In 1969 a lawsuit was filed against the Chicago Housing Authority alleging that Cabrini-Green was conceived and executed in a racially discriminatory manner that perpetuated racial segregation within neighbourhoods. In the film, Helen discovers that her white privileged world of the University and Lincoln Village and the crime-ridden, poverty-stricken Cabrini-Green are intrinsically linked: symbolically her apartment has the same layout as the housing project buildings. Also in chapter two, I discuss some of the social and political issues surrounding Cabrini-Green and the ways these are reflected in *Candyman*. Indeed, the boundaries between reality and fiction became even more blurred after the film's release when, in 1997, a child rapist 'haunting' the real Cabrini-Green was hunted down by gang members, much like the Candyman is in the film.

Chapter three gives a background to the production and reception of *Candyman*. Chapter four (*Candyman* and the Return of the Repressed) is devoted to textual analysis. The film at first appears to be a product of white liberal guilt at the plight of poor African-Americans; Helen, as previously noted, lives in an expensive apartment originally built as another part of the projects but later sold by the housing authority as a going concern and turned into designer condos. Likewise, Helen is seen working on her research at the University, while black menial workers toil as cleaners in the background well aware of the legend of the Candyman. However, Bernard Rose consciously invokes American history and the oppression of ethnic minorities in his backstory for Tony Todd's Candyman character: the origin of the Candyman is based on a public lynching and plays on the fear of retribution for the historical ill-treatment of African-Americans. Candyman/Daniel Robitaille was the son of a slave, a free man who came into money, schooled and brought up in polite society. His crime was that of miscegenation: he fell in love with a white girl, whom he made pregnant; his punishment was a horrible death, smothered in honey, stung to death by bees, his hand sawn off and replaced with a hook.

Candyman thus takes on an ambivalent, potentially reactionary inflection in its first half, as Helen is attacked by a black gang member brandishing a hook while she investigates the urban legend. We might be forgiven for thinking that the film is playing on fears of other cultures, of ethnic minorities, at this point. However, the film then shifts into transgressive mode when Helen eventually encounters the mythic Candyman, whose existence Helen has sought to debunk. The supernatural element takes over as Helen is drawn into the Candyman's world – and he into hers – and Helen is forced into complicity with the Candyman when she is blamed for the murders that he has committed. While the film suggests that the Candyman may indeed be a figment of Helen's imagination, it makes clear that empathy exists between them based on their mutual dispossession. As Linda Williams has commented, there is, in horror cinema, a strange affinity between monster and woman: both are Other to male normative sexuality and desire (1983: 63).

Helen's research into urban myths is her bid for recognition in the (as depicted in the film) patriarchal world of academia; her attempt to gain the respect of the men around her, including that of her own husband and doctoral supervisor, Trevor. Early in the film, Trevor introduces Helen to his students as his 'charming wife'; it is already suggested that he is having an affair; and when a senior academic denigrates Helen's research, Trevor does not stand up for her; instead he urges her not to rock the boat and threaten his good standing at the University. Helen's arrest and subsequent incarceration in a mental institution provides Trevor with an opportunity to move his younger student mistress into the apartment – a further betrayal of Helen's trust. Helen comes to realise that she

Director Bernard Rose (behind the camera) lines up a shot with Virginia Madsen for Candyman

is alone in a male-dominated world; now one of the dispossessed, she must learn to function independently of her husband, of the University, and ultimately, of her demon lover, the Candyman, in order to find vindication as a woman.

Of course, there are other ways to interpret the story, and also in chapter four I give some consideration to the idea of Helen becoming, in her resurrected avenging angel persona at the end of the film, an example of Creed's Monstrous-Feminine. I argue for the legitimacy of this viewpoint; however, I suggest that Rose's conclusion (which is supported by Barker) is meant to illustrate that no room exists within the current social order for the recognition of women, in the same way that none exists for impoverished blacks. The film takes on a cyclical form, as, in the final scene, Trevor suffers the same guilt over the unjust demise of Helen as whites felt for the plight of the African-American. He both fears and desires punishment for his guilt and complicity in Helen's oppression; and Helen appears from beyond the grave to administer retribution.

In a sense, Helen is already in a liminal state at the start of the film. As in the 'Bloody Mary' legend, what Helen really sees in the mirror as she summons the Candyman is a premonition of what she will become, an early 'recognition' of her dispossessed Other self. Helen's journey throughout the story is thus one of realisation and, ultimately, of transcendence. As Barker has commented of his work, 'it is the women who discover transcendence, who come into their own' (Cowan, 1992: 18).

For such a transgressive work, *Candyman* was a huge box office hit, grossing $25,792,310 (Box Office Mojo). In the final chapter (Sequels, Spin-offs and Knock-offs) I look at *Candyman: Farewell to the Flesh* and *Candyman: Day of the Dead* in terms of what they add to the *Candyman* mythos. Of the knock offs, I look at the various movies based on the legend of 'Bloody Mary', and the *Urban Legend* franchise, which includes the direct-to-DVD entry *Urban Legends: Bloody Mary* (2005). The continuing popularity of these films suggests that, in our culture, the urban myth – and what it represents – is still very much alive...

1. 'SWEETS TO THE SWEET': FROM 'THE FORBIDDEN' TO CANDYMAN

CLIVE BARKER: TRANSGRESSION AND TRANSCENDENCE

Clive Barker's lower-middle class background, like that of William Blake, partly accounts for his approach as a writer and visual artist: his tendency to rebel against the orthodox, to favour tradition above avant-gardism, and to follow his own instincts rather than the fashion or the 'norm'. Artists and painters who grow up with a lack of wealth and privilege are compelled to pursue their own paths, which often leads them to fly in the face of convention. William Blake began his career as an engraver rather than as a painter, and at the Royal Academy he railed against the then-fashionable style of Rubens; instead he championed the Classicism of Michelangelo and Raphael. Similarly, as a young artist, Barker declined a place at the Royal College of Art, feeling that he would have been 'trapped in an educational system that would have taught me a lot of things I didn't *need*. Or worse, it would have taught me nothing at all' (Snyder, 2009). Instead he chose the creative freedom of the 'dole' (as was an option for budding artists in the early '80s) and wrote short stories, plays, and eventually novels.

Barker's upbringing in a gritty Liverpool left a mark on his creative work in other ways too; his stated ambition, similar to that of Blake, is to take in 'heaven, hell and earth in between'. Even in his later fantasy novels, such as the *Abarat* series, there is an emphasis on worlds existing in parallel: the 'real' world must, for Barker, exist alongside the fantasy realm. Barker has expressed a dislike of much modern fantasy that adopts only a 'sub-Tolkien invented world', as well as small scale, domestic horror such as *Poltergeist* (1982) where the fantastical elements are reduced. Instead, in his own work, Barker starts with the domestic in order to 'open out the vistas. Then maybe you expand to take in another cosmos!' (Wells, 2002: 172-182).

For Barker fantastic art and literature thus express the possibility of transcending the limits of ordinary experience, not only for the characters of his films and stories, but for the everyday reader and viewer:

> It seems to me that this kind of art, or horror fiction, or horror films, is, at its best, giving us material to go into our dreams with. It is going to throw up images which are

going to represent the ways in which we contextualise our daily experience. Many of those are going to be confrontations with things that we forbid ourselves – forbidden sexual ideas or fantasies, fears about death, or anxieties that we cannot, or will not articulate. (Wells, 2002: 177)

Closely aligned to the notion of transcendence in Barker's work is transgression, sexual and otherwise. This has obvious links to Barker's own homosexuality and his desire, as a gay man, to shape the culture. Paul Wells writes that sadomasochism in Barker's work is used not only to draw together issues of brutality and eroticism, but to present perspectives outside social orthodoxy: "'horror'' comes out of the fear of a perverse yet partially desired experience of a marginalized or unknown "otherness"' (2002: 172). It is not surprising, then, as Wells comments, that Barker was, especially in his early career as a writer and director of horror fiction, drawn to the Gothic for its implied discourse of 'the attractiveness of the perverse and the transgressive' (2002: 172-173). Barker's *Hellraiser* (1987) is, of course, quintessential in this respect. Described by the novelist and *Hellbound: Hellraiser 2* (1988) actress Barbie Wilde (in an email to the author) as a 'sexually transgressive antidote to the new-Victorianism of 1980s Thatcherite Britain', *Hellraiser* introduced a new mythos to horror cinema in the S&M-oriented Cenobites whose leader Pinhead (Doug Bradley) is very much a monster from the psycho-sexual id (Barker took inspiration for the character from punk fashion, Catholicism and the S&M clubs he visited in Amsterdam and New York). Pinhead's spoken credo, repeated throughout *Hellraiser* and its various film sequels, spin-off comics and stories is the need to achieve 'sweet suffering' through the (self) infliction of abject pain.

Barker is not without his detractors. One of his most vociferous critics, Christopher Sharrett, considers *Hellraiser's* 'spectacle of excess' as simultaneous with a condemnation, rather than a celebration, of transgressive sexuality. For Sharrett (writing in 1993) Pinhead and his Cenobites are representative both of desire *and* repression:

[T]heir tired conflation of sadomasochism… with sexuality in general, associate erotic transgression with self-destruction, making these films very central to the AIDS cinema or, rather, that branch of commercial cinema advancing the scapegoating politics of the age of AIDS. (2015: 290)

Sharrett argues that Barker's presentation of sexual curiosity in the film is 'unequivocally repulsive and destructive', as rendered in the manifestations of *Hellraiser*'s demon underworld where characters are seen to be punished for their desires through the administration of torture devices (such as being ripped apart by hooks). For Sharrett, also, the grotesque sadomasochism of the Cenobites speaks to the media representation of 'postpunk nihilism that debunks the romance of transgression and resistance' (2015: 291).

It is difficult to deny that much of the transgressive impact of Pinhead has been lost in the frequency of his appearances over the years. Recent incarnations have sought recuperation for the character in the form of Pinhead's yearning for spiritual salvation and an opportunity to enter Heaven. Indeed, Barker's dependence on Christian mythology is itself problematic; as early as the novella *The Hellbound Heart* (1986) (which Barker adapted into *Hellraiser*), the Cenobites are referred to as 'demons', equating their transgression with evil; and the conflation of sadomasochism and 'Hell' has been inherent in the series from the very start, as reflected in the titles of the films (*Hellraiser*, *Hellbound*, *Hell on Earth*, etc.) Taken in these terms, of course, it becomes easy to associate sexual transgression with cynicism in Barker's work, rather than any genuine move towards transcendence: a cynicism that within neoconservative culture (in Sharrett's words) 'replaces class consciousness and critical analysis' (ibid.). Whether these criticisms can also be aimed at *Candyman* will be explored later in this book.

BERNARD ROSE – ROMANTICISM AND THE GOTHIC

Bernard Rose occupies an equally unique position in British cinema. Graduate of the National Film and Television School (where he studied alongside Terence Davis among others) he started his career as a pioneering music video director in the early 1980s, and moved briefly into TV drama before making his theatrical feature film debut with the fantasy *Paperhouse* in 1988. *Candyman* (his first film as screenwriter) took Rose to Hollywood where, after writing and directing an epic version of *Anna Karenina* (1997), he would go on to challenge the orthodoxy of the film business with *Ivansxtc*. Produced for less than $150,000 using a high definition digital camera (then cutting-edge technology) and eschewing the involvement of the studios, this adaptation of

Tolstoy's 'The Death of Ivan Ilyich' marked Rose as an iconoclast, although the industry has subsequently caught up, technologically at least, with filming digitally. Rose continued writing and directing independent features (many starring Danny Huston) and now functions as his own cinematographer. Since 2005, Rose has alternated a number of low budget horror films with a further series of Tolstoy adaptations (*The Kreutzer Sonata* [2008]; *Boxing Day* [2012] and *Two Jacks* [2013]). In between, Rose has also written and directed an adaptation of Howard Marks' autobiography *Mr. Nice* (2011) and the Paganini biopic *The Devil's Violinist* (2013) (he made the Beethoven biopic *Immortal Beloved* in 1994).

Although it is his work in the horror genre that is of particular interest here, the eclecticism of Bernard Rose is remarkable. Few British directors since Ken Russell have worked in such a broad range of genres, in such innovative ways. Indeed, (and although Rose is perhaps not an *enfant terrible* in the same manner as Russell) the similarities between the two filmmakers are worth noting.

There is, of course, the shared interest in classical music (Rose is an accomplished concert pianist and composer in his own right) and moreover the lives of the great composers, given frank treatment in the films of both directors. Then there is the essential *musicality* of the films themselves, the bold visuals, and the influence of Brechtian drama on the narrative. Both directors are able to combine realism and fantasy, stylistic flamboyance, excess and ambition. Both belong to a school of Romanticism in British cinema that also gave us Michael Powell and Emeric Pressburger, Lindsay Anderson, Derek Jarman, John Boorman and Nicolas Roeg (and a number of lesser-known directors such as Ian Sellar [*Venus Peter*, 1989; *Prague*, 1992; *The Englishman*, 2007] and Chris Newby [*Anchoress*, 1993; *Madagascar Skin*, 1995; *Dickens in London*, 2012]). Romanticism's dark side embraces fantasy, horror and the Gothic; it is therefore not surprising that Rose is drawn to these genres, as was Ken Russell and the other aforementioned directors.

Another characteristic of Romanticism is an unerring sense of place, as displayed in Rose's first theatrical feature, *Paperhouse*. In the film, a young girl called Anna (Charlotte Burke) dreams of a house that exists in an alternate reality, and discovers that by sketching the house and its inhabitants she can manipulate events in that parallel world.

She draws a boy at the window, and in her dreams she goes to him. They become friends. When the boy, who is called Marc (Elliot Spiers), falls ill, Anna attempts to change the course of her dreams by adding to the picture; ultimately reality and fantasy collide and Anna must let go of one to preserve the other. The film's depiction of parallel worlds recalls Barker's work, an important foundation for *Candyman*; it also evokes the fantasy of Lewis Carroll, C.S. Lewis and *Celine and Julie Go Boating* (1974). Although the theme is a magical one, Rose presents both worlds credibly. The 'real' world is present-day London, and we glimpse it only fleetingly in brief establishing shots during Anna's drive home from school or through the bedroom window of her mother's (Glenn Headley) flat, but we get a vivid sense of modernity in these transitory moments (as we do in *Candyman*). The world of the 'paperhouse' itself is equally vivid; sparely sketched in by Anna, we have the grey house standing alone on a moor, in splendid isolation, framed only by the grass and a blue sky. Its interior is equally bare. These images imprint themselves on the retina because of their very starkness.

Paperhouse *(1988)*

Dramatically, *Paperhouse* suffers from an inert script (by Matthew Jacobs), poor dubbing and weak performances. However, its relationship to *Candyman* – as well as the strength of Rose's visuals – gives it added interest, especially when it comes to the film's darker elements. Anna dreams of her father (Ben Cross) – silhouetted against a brooding sky – attacking the paperhouse with a hammer, a powerful image that prefigures Tony Todd's first appearance to Helen, as a silhouette in the enclosed parking lot in *Candyman*. And like the Candyman, Anna's dream father is vanquished by flames. The 'fear of the father' in *Paperhouse* (which anticipates thematically Joe Dante's *The Hole* [2009], another children's fantasy with dark elements) underscores the film's central theme of a child's shifting identification from one parent to the other; resolved only once Anna is able to express her sexual feelings for Marc. The film also speaks of Jung in terms of the universal unconscious; Marc and Anna are 'real' and contact one another in their dreams – another link to Barker and *Candyman*.

Self-reflexivity is a key motif of 2005's *Snuff-Movie*, Rose's first horror film after *Candyman*. Indeed, *Snuff-Movie* is as much a film *about* horror movies as its predecessor, perhaps even more so. Jeroen Krabbé plays Boris Arkadin, a reclusive horror director who invites a group of young actors to his mansion to audition them for a new film: a re-enactment of the murder of Arkadin's wife by a death cult. Capturing events on CCTV cameras secreted in the mansion, Arkadin appears to be staging a real-life snuff movie for the internet. In the film reality and fiction start to merge, until we are unsure where one starts and the other ends. The same members of the cult who killed Arkadin's pregnant wife make a re-appearance, as history literally seems to repeat itself; and in the very final scene, Rose stages a volte-face that makes us question all that has come before.

Snuff-Movie's self-reflexivity is followed through formally in Rose's adoption of a 'meta' mode of address which includes the use of surveillance footage, web cam, and alternating hand-held Dogme 95-style shooting with more conventional filming and lighting. It opens with a pastiche of a Hammer-type '60s heritage horror film, revealed to be an Arkadin production called 'The Premature Burial' (this may be a reference to Roger Corman's 1962 Poe adaptation). From there, Rose goes on to spoof a '70s home movie, shot by one of the cult gang, depicting a party in Arkadin's mansion which leads to the murder. This 'movie-within-a-movie-within-a-movie' opening is reminiscent of Norman J. Warren's *Terror* (1978) which starts in a similar manner and goes on to comment about the genre in a self-reflexive way comparable to Rose's film. Disconcertingly, the documentary-maker Nick Broomfield appears in *Snuff-Movie*, playing himself; more allusions to performativity in film-making.

The director's name 'Arkadin' is a sly in-joke too, and probably a reference to Orson Welles' *Mr. Arkadin* (1955) whose narrative theme of fragmented identity would echo ironically in *Mr. Arkadin*'s release: it exists in numerous different versions, none of which can be considered definitive. But Krabbé's character is more obviously based on the director Roman Polanski, and *Snuff-Movie* explicitly references the Manson Family murders in which Polanski's pregnant wife Sharon Tate was killed. Numerous writers have speculated on how Polanski's macabre films seem to reflect certain events in his life and vice versa. In *Snuff-Movie*, the notion of life imitating art becomes ever more complex, until the boundaries between the two become virtually indistinguishable. Indeed, *Snuff-Movie* opens with Arkadin intoning in voice-over that 'this is the most shocking, most explicit, most terrifying' film he has ever made, inviting us to see Krabbé as a stand-in for Rose himself, suggesting that *Snuff-Movie* may well have been intended as a comment on the huge success of the *Candyman* franchise. Rose, in fact, gives Arkadin a speech about evoking audience sympathy in horror that he himself delivered in *Candyman*'s 2005 DVD commentary:

> The difference between a horror film and an action film is that in an action film it's all about who you sympathise with. In an action film you sympathise with the killer. That's why I don't make action films – because they're immoral as far as I'm concerned. In a horror film, on the other hand, you sympathise with the victim. In a horror film it's all about waiting to be killed, and it's all about trying to stay alive, which to me seems a much more human objective.

We might also read *Snuff-Movie* as Rose's commentary on changing cinema technology. In Arkadin's mansion, one of the actors questions the legitimacy of the project ('Where's the crew? Where's the audience?') to which Arkadin replies that technology has erased the need for a crew, and that the internet will inevitably provide an audience. Ultimately, *Snuff-Movie* is about voyeurism in the age of live video streaming, and its implications for the censorship bodies, of which Rose has said in his DVD commentary:

> Why do you think reality TV has completely raped the drama schedules? No-one wants to look at stuff like *Dawson's Creek* anymore. No-one wants to see people all quaffed and lipglossed up. Ugly. It's not real. They've seen reality now on TV too much and on the internet. You start messing around on there – everything is so much more

Deranged director Boris Arkadin (Jeroen Krabbé) films the crucifixion of Wendy Jones (Lisa Enos) in Rose's disturbing Snuff-Movie *(2005)*

explicit. They're not going to be able to maintain the kind of MPAA controls on the content like that.

Made seven years later, *SX_Tape* (2013) is a companion piece of sorts to *Snuff-Movie* but is the more conventional and less interesting of the two. Possibly this is because Rose did not write it, and it lacks the intensity of his previous work. Like *Snuff-Movie* it is apparently semi-improvised, but carefully controlled, and comments on the impact of emerging digital video technology, this time in terms of amateur pornography.

Two LA art students Adam (Ian Duncan) and Jill (Caitlyn Folley) experiment with a digital camera, and find it turns them on to covert filming, exhibitionism, and filmed sex in public. When they break into an abandoned hospital that administered abortions to 'troubled' women, intending to film a sex tape there, Jill becomes possessed by the spirit of a patient who was sexually abused by a doctor at the hospital before she was lobotomised. While under the influence of the spirit, Jill exacts bloody retribution on two friends – Bobby (Chris Coy) and Ellie (Diana Garcia) – who come to join them in the hospital, and finally on Adam, who has filmed the whole thing. The film ends with Jill, still possessed, biting off the penis of a man with whom she later makes another sex tape.

Found-footage from the hospital of SX_Tape *(2013)*

Arriving at the tail-end of the found footage cycle, *SX_Tape* adheres to those conventions fairly rigidly: it opens with Jill's interrogation by the police captured on CCTV, as we learn of Adam's death and the mysterious disappearance of her friends, before cutting to the 'found footage' on Adam's camera which makes up the main body of the film. This is a familiar narrative device used in several previous found footage movies including *Cannibal Holocaust* (1980) and *The Blair Witch Project* (1999). *SX_Tape* also suffers from the usual implausibility of found footage movies: who edited the footage afterwards and why? Why does the protagonist continue to film even when s/he is him/herself in danger? A derivative central premise (Brad Anderson's superior *Session 9* [2001] also took place in an abandoned hospital and featured murders by a possessed individual) and the general feeling of déjà vu that accompanied *SX_Tape* (coming as it did after a number of other similar films such as *Grave Encounters* [2011]) also diminish the film. Certainly *SX_Tape* seems less concerned with providing audiences with the staples of the found-footage genre – suspense and jump scares – than it is with how Adam and Jill use the camera to test the boundaries of their relationship, suggesting other levels of meaning to the film. The exploitative nature of the sex tape itself is underexplored, however, and the parallels between Jill's predicament as a generally unwilling participant in Adam's fantasy and the sexual abuse of the hospital's women patients at the hands of male doctors are indistinctly drawn.

Two years after *SX_Tape*, Rose made the astonishing *Frankenstein* (2015), a modern day adaptation of Mary Shelley's classic that contains some of the writer-director's finest work. It arguably stands alongside James Whale's *Frankenstein* (1931), Hammer's *The Curse of Frankenstein* (1957) and the TV film *Frankenstein – The True Story* (1973) as one of the greatest and most powerful versions of the novel. The master stroke of Rose's adaptation is its setting in modern day America, which, ironically, allows Rose to stay truer to the spirit of Shelley's original than a more straightforward period piece would have. Its immediacy is not diluted by the trappings of period drama.

Told entirely through the consciousness of 'Monster' (Xavier Samuel), the film starts as he is 'born', created in a government laboratory by scientist Viktor Frankenstein (Danny Huston). Like a newly-delivered baby, Monster imprints on a mother figure, Viktor's wife, Marie (Carrie-Ann Moss) but when his body starts to corrupt due to a fault in his DNA, the scientists attempt to euthanise Monster, who exhibits enormous physical strength and escapes the facility. Alone and lost in a brutal downtown Los Angeles, Monster searches in vain for love and belonging but finds only pain and rejection. His first taste of freedom outside the laboratory is cut short when he is brought down by Taser and beaten up by security officers; later (in a brilliant spin on the drowning of 'Little Maria' in Whale's version) he rescues a child from water but is assaulted by the LAPD, and then by a vigilante mob brandishing sticks and clubs.

Monster is brutalised at every turn; his subsequent acts of violence toward society are as a result of this brutalisation. When a cop shoots the stray dog which Monster has adopted as a companion, Monster attacks the cop so viciously that the cop cries for his mother. 'Momma…' repeats Monster, bewildered and despairing at the cruelty of the world he has entered. Rose does not shy away from showing sickening brutality that is institutionalised (it is impossible to watch *Frankenstein* without thinking of actual beatings by police officers captured on mobile phones in America around the time of *Frankenstein*'s production); likewise, Monster's role as outcast is highlighted throughout. Whilst Boris Karloff's 1931 creature stood in for war veterans, unemployed homeless men and homosexuals increasingly persecuted as a result of the 'sex crimes' panics which swept the United States during the Depression, Rose's Monster is representative of the urban poor in modern America. His allegorical function is emphasised by his seeming indestructability: he repeatedly returns to life after attempts are made to kill him, seeking redress from a society that demonises him and others who are similarly disenfranchised.

Monster inevitably finds himself amongst LA's dispossessed, with the beggars and hookers, where he befriends a blind, homeless man called Eddie (Tony Todd) who shows him kindness for the first time. He begins to learn language and to understand the workings of a society divided by 'immense wealth and squalid poverty', where a person without rank or status is considered to be 'a vagabond or a slave, doomed to waste his powers for the profits of the chosen few'. Monster eventually comes to realise he has no place in such a society, even amongst its lowest echelons. 'If I cannot inspire love,' he resolves in desperation, 'I will cause fear.' Monster tracks down Viktor and Marie to their home, and watches through the window as they begin to make love: an ironic evocation of the primal scene that further excludes the artificial creature. The film ends, like *Candyman*, with a conflagration of Monster and the object of his desire; Monster immolates himself, and Marie, in a final act of love, protects Monster but loses her own life in the process.

Eddie (Tony Todd) and Monster (Xavier Samuel) homeless on the streets of LA in Frankenstein *(2015)*

'THE FORBIDDEN'

'The Forbidden', on which *Candyman* is based, originated in stories told to Clive Barker during his childhood. Although he professes not to have known the term 'urban legend' before writing 'The Forbidden', Barker's story revolves around that very notion. Barker first heard the variation of the well-known urban legend, 'The Hook', around the campfire as a boy scout, ('the hook-handed man who escapes the asylum and terrorises young couples in their cars') but just as influential on Barker's story – if not more so – was the warning given to him by his grandmother not to go into public toilets alone 'because there were men who went around public toilets and cut the genitals off little boys' (Schwarz, 2004b). It is possible that Barker's grandmother was recounting the story of William McDonald, a serial killer known as The Sydney Mutilator, who between 1961 and 1962 murdered a number of down-and-outs by luring them into dark places, including public toilets, and stabbed them to death before removing their sexual organs. McDonald was born in Liverpool in 1924 and migrated to Australia in the fifties, where he committed the crimes. The murders and McDonald's ensuing trial were widely publicised, and the Liverpool connection would no doubt have made him a talking point in that city circa 1963, when Barker was ten or eleven years old. In 'The Forbidden', Helen is told of an incident near a housing estate, whereby a mentally subnormal young man is accosted in a public toilet by a razor-wielding maniac who cuts off his genitals.

The conflation of paedophilia, homosexuality and psychopathy in the form of urban myth is actually quite common, and has contributed to a number of sex crime panics throughout the years, especially in the United States, where social upheaval during the Great Depression, and in later decades Cold War hysteria, spurred widespread cultural anxieties focusing on the figure of the sexual psychopath. Children are still routinely told not to speak to strangers even though the inherent notion that 'strangers only mean you harm' arguably carries an equally damaging subtext closely related to fear of the Other. Interestingly, Barker's original Candyman is depicted as a sadistic child murderer who uses his hook to penetrate his victims sexually before tearing them apart.

First published in Clive Barker's *Books of Blood*, Vol. 5, in 1985, 'The Forbidden' opens in a contemporary Liverpool housing estate called Spector Street. The estate is a picture of urban decay: vandalised, rubbish-strewn, festooned with abandoned burned-out cars. Barker apparently based Spector Street on council estates in Liverpool that 'look exactly like Cabrini-Green [in the film version]' (Schwarz, 2004b). After World War 2, in an attempt to solve the shortage of housing, councils engaged modern architects (such as Erno Goldfinger) to design high rise tower blocks where people were placed in perpendicular arrangements in order to conserve space. Although apartments in the Brutalist style are now regarded as classic and some are highly sought after, the 1960s/1970s urban tower block quickly became synonymous with crime and violence in the inner city. Barker remarks in his *Candyman* DVD commentary: 'It was a sociological disaster. It was an architectural disaster. And in the case of England it was a structural disaster: we had two or three of those places that simply collapsed, such as at Ronan Point' (Ronan Point in Newham, London partially collapsed in 1968 when a gas explosion destroyed one side of the building). Barker's story in this respect owes something to the '70s satire of J.G. Ballard's novel *High Rise* (1975; film adaptation 2015) and David Cronenberg's film *Shivers* (also 1975) that posited high rise apartment buildings as places of social degeneration (one might also include among these dystopias *A Clockwork Orange* [1962; film adaptation 1971], whose delinquent protagonist, Alex, lives in a futuristic block of flats).

Diane Long Hoeveler argues that Barker's political agenda is clearly liberal: he presents the Spector Estate as a 'dehumanizing concrete hell' in which poor people are forced to live (2007: 102). For Hoeveler, 'The Forbidden' has a specific political purpose: to reveal the class prejudice and institutionalised poverty that 'permeated and polluted British society' (2007: 103). If this is indeed the case, then that message is unveiled only gradually. The reader's initial impression is of Barker's clear disgust for the squalor of the place and its inhabitants: he states early on in the story that 'it was the people who had spoiled Spector Street'. 'The Forbidden' equates physical squalor with horror and repugnance extremely forcefully.

In Barker's original story, Helen is studying graffiti rather than urban myth, combining her academic disciplines: sociology and aesthetics. Barker, as we know, has described himself as a Jungian, in that he believes in the collective unconscious. We can see aspects of this in Helen's thesis: her aim is to find some unifying convention in the graffiti on the estate despite the many hands involved; a pattern or predominant motif beyond the sociological phenomena. Hence, the stage is immediately set for a paranormal element to co-exist alongside reality.

Helen has a second motive for her study: her desire to be taken seriously by the academic establishment, and by Trevor, her philandering husband. If the thesis gains some serious attention, then, in turn, so will she.

Told of the hook-handed killer by Anne-Marie, a single mother on the estate, Helen decides to investigate further, and learns of the toilet castration. Her colleagues dismiss these stories as urban myths, with no factual basis, which only spurs Helen on. However, on returning to the estate a third time, she finds the residents suddenly afraid, no longer the garrulous types they were previously. When she learns that Anne-Marie's baby has been murdered, seemingly by Anne-Marie herself, Helen goes to the police. She attends the child's funeral, and afterwards finds herself inexplicably drawn to an empty flat in which a huge portrait of the Candyman has been painted on the wall:

> He was bright to the point of gaudiness: his flesh a waxy yellow, his thin lips pale blue, his wild eyes glittering as if their irises were set with rubies. His jacket was a patchwork, his trousers the same. He looked, she thought, almost ridiculous, with his blood-stained motley, and the hint of rouge on his jaundiced cheeks. (Barker, 1985: 135)

Thus the Candyman of 'The Forbidden' is a taboo figure of a different kind to that which appears in the film. Here in Barker's original we have a perverse amalgam of sex offender and death incarnate. This Candyman, with his rouged jaundiced visage, is more Beast of Jersey[1] than noble savage. He is the spirit of the dark place that is the Spector Estate. Less a return of the repressed than he would become in Rose's version, the Candyman of Barker's tale is more a construction and reinforcement of the worldview of the housing estate residents in the story: their own degeneracy writ large.

As in the film, Helen gradually comes to identify with the residents of the estate and their disenfranchisement. Barker counterpoints Helen's disintegrating marriage and her humiliation by her male academic colleagues with her repeat visits to the estate: in doing so, Barker shifts our sympathies closer toward the council estate people, away from the 'educated fools' of the University. Both worlds are referred to in the story as 'wastelands', and Helen moves from 'one wasteland to another'. It is true that in Barker's early short stories a sense of despair and disgust lingers over humanity in general. There are few truly sympathetic characters in *The Books of Blood*. The misanthropic tone of the stories has generally carried over into the film adaptations made of them (*Rawhead Rex*, 1986; *The Midnight Meat Train*, *Book of Blood*, 2008; *Dread*, 2009). The Helen of 'The Forbidden' never discovers her own inner reserve as Virginia Madsen's character does in *Candyman*. However, she does come to regard Spector Street as her spiritual 'home'.

In the Barker story, the spirit of the estate's dispossessed – the Candyman – claims Helen as his own. As in the film he offers her immortality in return for her life, as an urban myth like himself, to be dead, but remembered everywhere; immortal in gossip and graffiti, 'to live in people's dreams; to be whispered at street-corners'. Helen, of course, refuses the offer. She follows Anne-Marie to a bonfire built by the residents of Spector Street for Guy Fawkes celebrations (another kind of urban legend and ritual destruction). After Anne-Marie secretes the body of her dead baby in the bonfire, Helen climbs inside to retrieve it (presumably so that the truth can be revealed to the authorities). However, the Candyman appears to her inside the bonfire and draws her into the flames after the bonfire is lit by the residents. In Barker's version, Helen dies in the fire, but the suggestion remains that she might become, in time, 'a story with which to frighten children'. In 'The Forbidden', as Diane Long Hoeveler acknowledges:

> Barker is telling another, more cryptic and much darker tale, and it concerns the human need to invent divinities that embody our worst fears and imaginings. Candyman, the stranger is somehow another version of Christ the redeemer, the superhuman who holds out the promise of sweets but delivers instead only the stinking tomb. (2007: 105)

FOOTNOTES

1.   Serial sex offender Edward Paisnel, AKA 'The Beast of Jersey', terrorised the Channel Island of Jersey between 1960-1971, breaking into homes at night dressed in a black wig and rubber mask to attack women and children.

2. URBAN LEGENDS, URBAN MYTHS: ADAPTING *CANDYMAN*

Clive Barker contends that when he wrote 'The Forbidden' in 1985 he was unaware of the term 'urban legend'. Social scientists and folklorists have theorised that urban legends create and reinforce the worldview of the group within which they are told, sometimes through the acting out of the legends themselves in various forms of ostension (Koven, 1999). Folklorists Dégh and Vászony discuss how, for instance, urban legends of Halloween candy laced with razorblades led to actual incidents of sweets contaminated by needles and razors; the urban myth itself became ritually acted out. Similarly, the legend of Guy Fawkes and the Gunpowder Plot has become a staple of British culture, ritually re-enacted each November 5th. Indeed, *Candyman*, the film, created its own 'myth' and ostension (Barker tells of at least one academic who assumed the Candyman was an actual urban legend and not just a figment of Barker's imagination). Several years after the release of the film, a child rapist 'haunting' the real Cabrini-Green estate in Chicago was hunted down by gang members, much like the Candyman is in the film. (In 1997 nine-year-old Shatoya Currie was raped, beaten and left for dead in a stairwell. Her attacker, a known sex offender by the name of Patrick Sykes, had sprayed her with gang symbols in an attempt to throw the police off his trail. The crime so appalled the Cabrini-Green community that the local gangs worked with the police to find the girl's assailant.)

Despite Barker's then-unawareness of the term, a number of classic urban myths already appear in 'The Forbidden', including the tale of the hook, razorblades in sweets and the public toilet castration. Bernard Rose would develop the self-reflexive aspects of the story in his adaptation, the sense that the story is very much about itself, about the experience of horror and the nature of campfire storytelling. Mikel J. Koven enumerates the various contemporary legends eventually used in the film:

> [M]otifs which make up the diegesis of the film, are not limited to [the] fusion of 'beauty and the beast' with 'the hook-handed killer' and the ritual of 'Mary Worth'. Other demonstrated contemporary legends include 'Razor Blades Found in Halloween Candy' (Candyman is presumably responsible for that), 'Child Emasculated in Public Washroom', and even the traditional British legend of Gelert. Other

contemporary legends are presented within the diegesis rhetorically (they are told within the narrative): the 'Hippie Babysitter', who cooks the child instead of the turkey, and 'Alligators in the Sewers', to name but two. (1999: 157)

Indeed, *Candyman*'s producer Alan Poul asserts in the film's DVD commentary that the film 'tries to be a kind of compendium of the entire phenomenon of urban legends, and then tries to say, let's take this one and let's just say that it's true'. As I have previously commented, *Candyman* starts out as Helen's investigation into urban myth; eventually the film becomes about the nature of urban myth itself. The film interrogates the idea of urban myth, and at the same time appropriates actual urban legends such as 'Bloody Mary'. Rose admits in the DVD commentary:

The urban legend that most influenced me that was not in the short story that I actually found in Chicago was the legend of Bloody Mary; if you say Bloody Mary's name in the mirror thirteen times, she'll appear and do you. I borrowed that for the Candyman.

The legend of Bloody Mary first emerged in the 1960s as an adolescent party game, although it didn't start to be recorded by folklorists until the 1970s. In the most popular retellings of the legend, Mary Worth (known also as Mary Worthington and/or Mary Whales) is a beautiful but vain girl who suffers an accident so terrible that it leaves her disfigured (modern variations usually involve her in a fatal car crash). Her spirit enters the mirror that enchanted her when she was alive and beautiful. If you say her name in the bathroom mirror, Mary's ghost will appear in the reflection to haunt and/or kill you (in some versions Mary will show you the future and/or disclose the name of the person you will marry). The Bloody Mary legend seems to hold particular meaning for pre-pubescent girls (David Emery describes it as akin to a coming-of-age ritual 'warning girls of what to expect on attaining puberty [2016]) and the legend continues to be disseminated via internet chat rooms and social network sites; indeed the Bloody Mary 'curse' is regularly sent in chain letter emails, text messages and social media postings intended to traumatise adolescents (see chapter 5 for further discussion of 'Bloody Mary' in recent teen horror films).

Another direct influence on Rose when he was writing the screenplay for *Candyman* was a book by Jan Harold Brunvand entitled *The Vanishing Hitchhiker* (now considered a foundational work in the study of urban legends). Brunvand asserts that urban myths present themselves as true accounts of real-life experiences; realistic stories with an ironic or supernatural twist. Brunvand considers urban legends an integral part of Anglo-American culture; their word-of-mouth dissemination is aided and validated by the mass media, but they are, he stresses, folklore, not oral history. The narrative structures of urban myths dispel them as literal accounts of actual events. Urban legends, according to Brunvand, are simply additional instances of living folklore. 'Still,' Brunvand writes, 'like traditional folklore, these stories do tell one kind of truth. They are a unique, unselfconscious reflection of major concerns of individuals in the society in which the legends circulate' (1981: xii).

Despite the myriad of re-tellings, embellishments and re-localisations ('it happened a few years ago near Moses Lake in Indiana… My room-mate's boyfriend knew him') the basic narratives remain the same. A standard rule of folk-narrative plot is that a taboo must be broken (an 'interdiction violated'): many urban legends are, at their most basic, cautionary tales that stress the dangers of transgressing social norms. Brunvand argues that for legends to survive in our culture as living folklore, they must contain three essential elements: a strong basic story appeal, a foundation in actual belief and a meaningful message or 'moral'. The primary message may consist of an explicit warning, or an example of poetic justice; however, secondary meanings are often present, suggested metaphorically or symbolically; according to Brunvand, 'these may provide deeper criticism of human behaviour or social conditions' (1981: 11). Furthermore, for an urban legend to be retained within the culture, it must fulfil a genuine need, one of the most common being 'to show that the prosaic contemporary scene is capable of producing shocking or amazing occurrences' which nevertheless are explainable in logical terms (1981: 12).

Part of *Candyman*'s narrative strategy is that it apparently 'explains' the nature of the Candyman legend that Helen is investigating, giving a logical reason for the Cabrini-Green murders: they are the work of a hoaxer who, in acts of pseudo-ostension, pretends to be the Candyman in order to keep the residents of the estate afraid. However, the film then debunks the rationality of which Brunvand speaks in order to ask: what if urban legends were actually real?

Numerous horror movies before *Candyman* resembled *in themselves* urban myths: *Halloween* (1978) and *The Burning* (1981), for example. However, in developing the urban legend motif of 'The Forbidden' self-reflexively – by making Helen's study of urban myth part of the actual plot – *Candyman* ultimately becomes a movie about horror movies – a monster movie about monsters. Rose appropriates Barker's general 'meta-fiction' approach to horror narrative ('why we write these tales, why we hear these tales') but manages to take it much further cinematically than Barker himself might have: *Candyman* is paradoxically a greater adaptation of Barker's work than Barker's own films of his novels to date. As Kim Newman noted in his review of *Candyman* for *Sight and Sound* (March, 1993), in adapting and elaborating on 'The Forbidden', Rose did 'an even more skilful job of translating Barker's singular approach to the screen than the author himself achieved in *Hellraiser* and *Nightbreed* (1990)'.

ADAPTING 'THE FORBIDDEN'

Above all, *Candyman* illustrates that as a screenwriter Rose is a master of the screen adaptation. In adapting 'The Forbidden', he was able to take the thematic material of the original story, expand it, and add something of his own, much as he has with his subsequent film adaptations. As Kim Newman remarked in his *Sight and Sound* review, Rose's screenplay of *Candyman* brilliantly combines 'the archetypal ingredients of the horror genre – knee-jerk shocks, stalking bogeyman, touches of dark humour – but also locates the horrors in an identifiable and credible landscape of urban decay' (1993).

Rose first became aware of 'The Forbidden' in 1989 after meeting Clive Barker at Pinewood Studios where Barker was shooting *Nightbreed*. Barker and Rose shared the same agent at CAA, Jay Moloney, who sent Rose an adaptation of 'In the Flesh', Barker's story in *The Books of Blood*, Vol. 5. Rose preferred 'The Forbidden', from the same volume. As Rose comments on the *Candyman* DVD, 'it had this really interesting shape to it'. Barker agreed to option 'The Forbidden' to Rose, who took it to Steve Golin at Propaganda Films. By 1990, Propaganda had become one of the most successful music video companies in the industry and was branching out into film and TV production with such notable titles as John Dahl's neo-noir *Kill Me Again* (1989), David Lynch's *Twin Peaks* (1990-91) and *Wild at Heart* (1990), and John Mackenzie's biopic of Lee Harvey

Oswald's killer, *Ruby* (1992). Golin agreed to pay for the development of a screenplay of *Candyman*, which he assumed Rose would write as well as direct. Rose had never written a screenplay before but accepted the hyphenate role. After reading the first draft, Golin agreed to finance the film on the strength of Rose's script.

Barker's creative input as executive producer was, by his own admission, less than that of Rose as the film's writer-director. The two agreed that because the film was being financed with American money (ultimately Polygram) the story would need to be relocated to the United States. However, it was Rose's decision to set the film in Chicago, having attended a film festival there and become fascinated by the city's architecture:

> Chicago seemed like a very dynamic place. So I went there to do some research, looking for a setting for the film, and that is how I came across the real housing project at Cabrini-Green. (Schwarz, 2004b)

As a British writer, Rose was unfamiliar with the speech patterns of Chicago people, and, as he told the Writers Guild of America in 2002, he undertook his research trips also with the purpose of learning 'how people would speak':

> When you are unfamiliar with how people sound, sometimes it makes you work harder to make them sound right. People are often very nervous about going into an unfamiliar background, but I believe that's the wrong thing to worry about. If the story is good and the scenes are good, you can find out how people speak and get that right.

The setting and the people: at some point in his research trips this conjunction suggested to Rose that the ethnic identity of the Candyman would need to be readdressed. Indeed, as Rose has remarked, 'the whole point about the Candyman is that he is a representative of people who are oppressed' (Schwarz, 2004b). However, as Rose understood, rigid demarcations of oppressed minorities are less useful in defining difference than the intersection of such groups: 'In American society the class barriers are drawn along racial lines, especially in a place like Chicago' (ibid.). This led Rose to make the decision that the Candyman should be black, and that race, gender and class would all be factors in the film's depiction of oppression.

Although he represents oppressed peoples, the Candyman himself would be sophisticated, educated and elegant; placing him within the lineage of the Gothic villain – Frankenstein, Dracula, the Phantom of the Opera – ultimately a tragic figure. However, his sexual overtures to Helen – a white woman – would play on cultural fears of the 'Mandingo', the well-endowed black man who seeks to mate with white women. American cinema has explored this stereotype in *Mandingo* (1975) and *Drum* (1976), as well as in Blaxploitation pictures such as *Shaft* (1971). Indeed, Blaxploitation horror films like *Blacula* (1972), *Blackenstein* (1973) and *Dr. Black, Mr. Hyde* (1976) serve as interesting precursors to *Candyman*. Although these films now tend to be dismissed as camp, they did at least allow African-American audiences to see themselves represented on screen, even if commentators are divided over whether or not those representations are racist. Harry Benshoff has argued that many Blaxploitation horror films 'reappropriated the mainstream cinema's monstrous figures for black goals, turning vampires, Frankenstein monsters, and transformation monsters into agents of black pride and black power' (2000: 37). Others consider the films simply offer variations on traditional genre norms, with black actors taking the roles usually occupied by whites, but without any fundamental subversion or reworking of generic formula. Critics of Blaxploitation claim that the representation of race in these films is inauthentic. Certainly, Blaxploitation films were products of the predominantly white film industry; intended for an African-American urban audience but designed also to cross-over to white audiences.

At the heart of *Candyman* is the taboo issue of miscegenation: a key concern of race horror that predates even Blaxploitation. As Peter Hutchings points out, in the early history of the horror genre, blackness tended to be shown in terms of 'primitivism and exoticism' (2004: 110). The emphasis, particularly in the horror films of the 1930s and 1940s, was on non-American blacks, while African-American characters were seen only occasionally on-screen, often as comic relief. In *White Zombie* (1932) and *I Walked with a Zombie* (1943) the black characters encountered by whites in exotic locales have been said to represent white colonialist fears of subservient peoples rising up against their masters. Black and white interbreeding, meanwhile, played out in coded form, often in the pairing of gorilla and white girl – a genre staple in the 1920s and 1930s – in such movies as *The Gorilla* (1927), *Ingagi* (1930) and *Murders in the Rue Morgue* (1931).

HELEN
BLACKS
OUT.

Bernard Rose's storyboards for Candyman

King Kong is, of course, a prime example, and, for this reason, must stand as another precursor to *Candyman*. Indeed, Bernard Rose, in his candid DVD commentary to *Candyman* remarks that the Candyman's attack is openly sexual:'he had basically this huge cock in his hand. And he kills people by sticking it in them, in their orifices. It's part of the appeal of the movie. I think it's partly why people like it.'

Propaganda was nervous about casting a black actor as the Candyman because they feared it might be seen as racist. Indeed, Rose was asked by company executives to meet with the NAACP (National Association for the Advancement of Colored People) to discuss the script and its representation of Candyman as a black character within it:

> I had to go and have a whole set of meetings with the NAACP, because the producers were so worried, and what they said to me when they'd read the script was 'Why are we even having this meeting? You know, this is just good fun.'Their argument was 'Why shouldn't a black actor be a ghost? Why shouldn't a black actor play Freddy Krueger or Hannibal Lector? If you're saying that they can't be, it's really perverse.This is a horror movie...' (Jackson, 1993)

Nevertheless, *Candyman* did cause controversy amongst some African-American filmmakers at the time of its production because of its representation of blackness. The director Carl Franklin (*One False Move* [1992] *Devil in a Blue Dress* [1995]) was offended by the Candyman's obsession with a white woman, which he, in fact, likened to *King Kong*, claiming that black women become non-entities in such films. Franklin also objected to the Candyman exacting revenge on his own community, which he claimed reinforces perceptions of blacks against blacks.'There's no question that this film plays on white middle-class fears of black people,' Franklin remarked.'It unabashedly uses racial stereotypes and destructive myths to create shock' (Lovell, 1992).

The Chicago Tribune ran a story about the film's production ('Black Slasher *Candyman* Draws Fire Over "Racist" Depictions', October 29, 1992) raising similar concerns about the film's representations of black people. It listed a number of aspects of the screenplay which it claimed could be seen as perpetuating racist myths:

- The boogyman (played by 6-foot-5 Tony Todd) is hulking, bloodthirsty and black.
- Black men, like the mournful Candyman, are obsessed with white women.

- The black man's anger toward the white Establishment is usually vented on his own race. (Though tortured and killed by a white mob in 1890, Candyman preys mostly on black women and children, whom he guts and mutilates with his hook.)

- The black community is made up not of individuals but of amorphous faces that exact in-kind revenge or pay tribute en masse (like the chorus in 1943's *Cabin in the Sky*). (ibid.)

The Chicago Tribune was concerned by how the screenplay seemed to represent the black community in the Cabrini-Green apartment complex as susceptible to superstition and urban myth; that the projects were depicted in the script as a 'ready-made house of horrors, guarded by gang members and overrun by crack addicts'; and that Cabrini-Green was described (in distributor TriStar's press kit) as 'a hopeless community ... a ghetto filled with poverty, despair and violence'. Such representations, the newspaper reasoned, carried the risk of perpetuating the most damaging myths and stereotypes affixed to the inner city.

THE REAL CABRINI-GREEN

Synonymous with crime and gangs, the Cabrini-Green projects had, at the time of *Candyman*'s production, become a symbol for the worst of public housing in the United States. Over the years sensational news accounts of shootings, drug dens and gang violence had painted a disturbing picture of the projects, one that diminished stories of the suffering and chaos that residents endured at the hands of the Chicago Housing Authority whose policies effectively turned the projects into ghettoes.

Situated on the Near North Side, Cabrini-Green was originally constructed as a low-rise apartment complex for workers during World War 2; at that time the population was ethnically mixed, comprising poor Italians, Puerto Ricans, Irish and African-Americans. High-rise extensions to the projects were built in the late 1950s and early 1960s as a response to the population boom, but by the mid-'60s racial segregation had set in and Cabrini-Green's population had become predominantly black. In 1966, a lawsuit was filed by community organiser and activist Dorothy Gautreaux against the Chicago Housing Association alleging that its public housing policies were racially discriminatory and perpetuated racial segregation. In 1969, the CHA was found liable by Federal Judgement Order. The success of the Gautreaux lawsuit prohibited the CHA from constructing any further projects in predominantly African-American areas of the city.

By then, following the assassination of Martin Luther King Jr. in April 1968, riots had enveloped Chicago; and Cabrini-Green, due to its geographical proximity to the wealthy Gold Coast and Lincoln Park neighbourhoods had been strictly cordoned off. This marked a turning point for the projects. Subsequent federal housing policy reforms prioritising the homeless and single mothers, although well-intentioned, reduced the CHA's rental income; at the same time, the most disadvantaged Chicago citizens were being moved into public housing in increasing numbers; and the already incompetent CHA stopped maintaining Cabrini-Green due to lack of funds. The projects quickly became run-down and squalid; vandalism increased. This created an impression of urban decay, and Cabrini-Green's worsening reputation was seized upon by the media as an example of the failure of public housing in America.

Yet the sensationalised news accounts of delinquency and squalor in Cabrini-Green failed to highlight the tenant activism and community action of the residents, most of whom were families. Many residents grouped together to support and protect each other, and to protest against the negligence of the CHA. Indeed, the success of the Gautreaux case created a legacy that affected public housing policy not only in Chicago, but across the US, bringing an end to public housing high rises and expanding housing opportunities for public housing families; it led to the construction of more housing for mixed-income communities and brought about an end to racial discrimination in public housing policy. (Cabrini-Green itself was largely demolished by 2011 to make way for redevelopment.) American popular culture tends to overlook positive tenant activism in its representations of inner city public housing and its residents; the power of the (black, working-class) collective, and of cooperative social endeavour generally, is less championed by the media than messages of competition and self-actualisation, and undercurrents of racial and class discrimination remain in depictions of indolent poor blacks being themselves to blame for their situation.

An aerial view of Cabrini-Green in Candyman

In his assessment of *Candyman*, Peter Hutchings argues that the narrative of the film, although containing an element of social critique, moves away from explicit political engagement with social issues. This occurs most tellingly, according to Hutchings, when *Candyman* invokes the idea of Cabrini-Green's working-class black community as 'an oppositional force'. At the end of the film, a procession of Cabrini-Green residents, led by Anne-Marie, appears unexpectedly at Helen's funeral. However, the film has given no indication of how this collectivity has come about: all we have been shown of Cabrini-Green, Hutchings suggests, is that it is beset by drug taking and violence, and is a world devoid of the will or the means to organise itself politically. Thus, the final collective of residents at Helen's funeral becomes an overtly rhetorical device used by the filmmakers as 'a gesture towards political significance and social relevance rather than a systematic and politically aware engagement with issues to do with racial and class divisions' (2004: 125). Such a 'communal' moment in *Candyman* – and in other race horror films like *The People Under the Stairs* (1991) – Hutchings concludes, may signify the oppressiveness and complacent arrogance of the well-off white characters, but does so in a moralistic way 'with this criticism delivered primarily through the presence of a group of the "oppressed" poor and black who themselves have little or nothing to say about their own situation' (ibid.).

One might attempt to defend *Candyman* in this respect by suggesting that Anne-Marie can be read as an organiser or a Dorothy Gautreaux figure. In the screenplay, she is given an oppositional voice: it is made clear that she has built a home for herself and her child in Cabrini-Green, and she initially challenges Helen on her study: 'What you gonna say? That we're bad, we steal, we gangbang, we do drugs?' However, it is difficult to refute Hutchings' point that *Candyman* ultimately leads us away from any explicit political engagement with social issues. As Bernard Rose says himself:

> *Candyman*'s thrust is metaphysical instead of political. My element of social criticism asks how people can be expected to live in squalor, because the housing authority has allowed Cabrini-Green to rot instead of trying to maintain it. But *Candyman* really poses the question that if God exists because we believe in him, what would happen if the worship ceased? Would there be a five-minute period where God is running on belief, and would he try to win his followers back? (Schweiger, 1992: 12)

Indeed, if *Candyman* contains any further thrust as social critique, it might best be detected in the film's sly commentary on white people's fear of blackness, of which the real Cabrini-Green serves as an example. In order to expand the narrative to feature film length, Rose's adaptation of 'The Forbidden' utilised what Roger Ebert described in his review of *Candyman* as 'Hitchcock's favourite formula, the Innocent Victim Wrongly Accused': Helen is 'set up' by the Candyman as the key suspect in the murder investigation, thereby isolating her from her complacent middle-class existence. Moreover, the film suggests that the Candyman is merely a figment of Helen's imagination. This evocation of paranoia is one of the film's most powerful elements. As Rose has stated in his DVD commentary, 'in a sense it's a story about (Helen) losing her mind. You can interpret the story as there being no Candyman.' In this way, *Candyman* becomes a commentary on fear, specifically white middle-class fear of 'the wrong part of town, being caught where some threatening activity is going to come out and get you'. As Rose observes, such irrational fear is fundamental to racism, and is also 'poverty motivated'. Therefore *Candyman* becomes for Rose 'a subtle way of actually exploring what is really the dark heart of American history, which is: a country built on slavery'. The film resonates with this subtext, presenting in allegorical form an historical truth that has been erased from most official discourses on modern America:

There are two big blots on American history. The first was the massacre of the native Americans. The second was slavery. Essentially, those two events aren't tangential to American history: they *are* the real history of America. (Bernard Rose, *Candyman* DVD commentary, 2005)

3. *CANDYMAN*: PRODUCTION AND RECEPTION

CASTING

The casting of *Candyman* commenced in 1991, after Propaganda and Polygram greenlit the film with a budget of $7m. It is often claimed that Eddie Murphy was the initial choice for the Candyman role, but this is itself a myth (Murphy would later star in Wes Craven's 1995 comedy-horror flop *Vampire in Brooklyn*). Bernard Rose had seen Tony Todd in Joseph Sargent's *Ivory Hunters* (1990) (aka *The Last Elephant*), a made-for-TV movie about the ivory trade filmed in Nairobi, and had been struck by his voice, height and aristocratic air which fit Rose's conception of the character. Indeed, Rose's initial drawings of the Candyman resembled Todd closely.

A classically trained actor, Todd (born in 1954) had forged a career on the New York stage performing plays by Shakespeare, Eugene O'Neill and August Wilson; Oliver Stone spotted him in Dalton Trumbo's anti-war polemic, *Johnny Got His Gun*, and brought him to Hollywood for *Platoon* (1986). Todd became associated with cult science-fiction TV in *Star Trek: The Next Generation* (1990) (over the years he would also appear in *Deep Space Nine* and *Voyager*). His first iconic role in a horror film, however, was playing the protagonist Ben in Tom Savini's 1990 remake of *Night of the Living Dead*. Todd's casting in that film emphasises both the continuity of the remake with the original and its areas of departure from the source film. Todd's Ben is dignified and educated, much like the character played by Duane Jones in the 1968 version; however, in keeping with the foregrounding of the first film's social commentary (which involves a more pronounced critique of family breakdown and reflection on feminism and racial inequality) Todd's Ben is also angrier. Significantly, then, Tony Todd holds the distinction of playing two of the most important black characters in modern horror cinema.

On his role in *Candyman*, however, Todd has commented that it has been both a blessing and a curse: 'It's great to make a movie that really rattles people, but at the same time, as actors, we spend a lot of time trying to distance ourselves from that particular image' (Schwarz, 2004b). Todd's primary inspiration for the Candyman was Lon Chaney's performance in *Phantom of the Opera* (1925) in terms of the alienation, pain and tragic dimension of the character. Although Todd only appears in the first film for a total of eight minutes, he saw the role as an opportunity to raise race issues and increase the visibility of black actors in Hollywood; to give tribute to African-American actors and filmmakers who 'for whatever limitations didn't get to make a film or finish or have a frame from A-Z' (ibid.) The film's success raised Todd's profile significantly, and when it came to the sequel *Candyman: Farewell to the Flesh*, he was involved in developing the screenplay with Bill Condon (writer-director of *Gods and Monsters* [1998] *Kinsey* [2004] *Dreamgirls* [2006] *The Twilight Saga: Breaking Dawn* [2011/2012] *Mr Holmes* [2015], *Beauty and the Beast* [2017]), emphasising the themes of racism in the scenario:

> All that back story in the second one: that was my stuff. How he was an artist and the fact that his father was a cobbler. Because I wanted it rooted in something. It wasn't just slash slash, kill kill, you know? And I wanted it to address the segregation laws, which is one of the nation's greatest tragedies, where a black man could be shot on sight for being seen with a white woman. (Cooper, 2014)

Todd admits that there are regressive aspects in the pop culture phenomenon of *Candyman*. He is troubled by certain elements of the film's audience: *Candyman* is popular with inner city gang members and with redneck horror fans in the South, for example ('I've had full Klan members come up to my table and say, "I love the way you kill people"' (ibid.)). But, equally, he has used the film's popularity with gangs to facilitate his work as an interventionist. Todd grew up on the edge of housing projects, and as a teenager would smuggle books past local gangs in his desire to have an education as opposed to joining a gang. In interviews, Todd remains outspoken about both the continuing racial divisions in America and the institutionalised racism inherent in the housing projects of the past, describing Cabrini-Green to *Bloody Disgusting* as 'modern day indentured slavery through the power of crack, which was created by the government' (ibid.). Todd is also sceptical about Cabrini-Green's demolition to make way for upmarket housing, citing gentrification rather than social progress as one of the reasons behind the redevelopment of the projects (indeed many residents of Cabrini-Green complained that, during redevelopment, families were displaced from their homes without being rehoused, and that the CHA reneged on its promise to redevelop Cabrini-Green as 100% public housing). As Todd points out, Cabrini-Green was demolished at least partly because it was close to the wealthy Chicago districts: 'And the weird thing is they coexisted, because it was two different worlds and never the two shall meet, except for the downtown people who had to go to Cabrini-Green to get their fix' (ibid.). On working with gangs as a result of *Candyman*, Todd has said:

> One positive thing I've been able to do, because gang members love that film so fucking much, I get a lot of work as a gang interventionist. We use *Candyman* to open up a dialogue and we talk about things. One of my dream projects is a foundation where teenagers from different backgrounds can be taken someplace every year. Just get them together and see that there's a different world out there. Talk to them about the disparities between cultures and classes in this society, you know? And hopefully they come back home and spread whatever joy they got. I want that to be my legacy. (ibid.)

Candyman's legacy in terms of Virginia Madsen's subsequent career has also been significant. The role of Helen Lyle has been career-defining for the Chicago-born actress and producer, who previous to *Candyman*, was best known 'for being beautiful, for being sexy, for being sultry' (Schwarz, 2004b) in such films as David Lynch's *Dune* (1984) and Dennis Hopper's *The Hotspot* (1990). Madsen's own website (http://virginia-madsen. org/) describes her as 'a cool, classic beauty, with a vibrant blonde mane'; however, Helen provided a character of serious intellect, a lead role, and an opportunity to move outside of Hollywood typecasting. 'I was never worried about being typecast,' Madsen claims, 'I was only one role away from being out of that. But [before *Candyman*] I was having trouble getting that role' (Schwarz, 2004b).

Madsen had been married to Danny Huston at the time of *Candyman*, and Bernard Rose knew her socially. Sandra Bullock was also reportedly considered for Helen, but Rose had always been interested in Madsen for the role, despite reservations about her screen persona of beauty and glamour:

> Bernard didn't really see me as Helen. I had to kind of grow into that. Bernard saw me as being too beautiful. He knew that I was a smart woman, that I was strong, that I was from Chicago, that I was down to earth, but physically he saw me as glamorous. (DVD commentary, 2005)

In order to make her look more 'real', Madsen underwent something of a make-over for the role, although not to the extent of uglifying her in the kind of sensationalised way that would later become fashionable in Hollywood biopics (Nicole Kidman as Virginia Woolf in *The Hours* [2002]; Charlize Theron as Aileen Wuornos in *Monster* [2003]). Madsen gained weight, cut her hair and appeared without make-up for the most part. The effect was to make Madsen (who was thirty-years old at the time of filming) look younger, more believable as a graduate student; however, the 'puppy-fat' look of Helen also serves to emphasise her journey around which the film is structured: from naïve child-woman to experienced fully-grown woman. Playing Helen enabled Madsen to find herself as an actress (Madsen's Maya in *Sideways* [2004] is, in some ways, an older, wiser version of the character) and, in a sense, may have helped her find herself as a woman at that particular point in her life. Rose developed the character from Clive Barker's story, focusing on her disintegrating marriage and her desire to gain validation through her academic study of urban myths. As Rose notes in the *Candyman* DVD commentary:

I think the important thing about Helen as a character is that she's in an unhappy marriage, she's looking for something that's going to engage her, she sort of feels trapped, I think, and although she shifts the blame onto her husband, as him being the one who's unfaithful, in a sense, if you look at her from the very beginning she's kind of slightly dislocated from her marriage, from her world; she's looking for something.

Helen is the film's structuring character, but more than that, she provides the audience-identification figure of *Candyman*. Rose deliberately stays with her throughout the film; the story is filtered through Helen's consciousness. No scene takes place outside of that. Horror films – as Rose has pointed out – happen very much in the 'present tense'; and many scenes in *Candyman* are designed by Rose to create empathy between the audience and Madsen/Helen:

It's about existential things: her sitting there in the bath, feeling uneasy, her getting a beer out of the fridge, her just walking around taking pictures. I really wanted to try and keep the audience being with her in the present tense throughout the movie. (ibid.)

The film builds towards Helen's confrontation with the truth: about her marriage, about the Candyman, about racial segregation, and about herself as a woman and her own subjugation within the social order. As Rose comments:

CANDYMAN

She's trying to solve a mystery, and she's trying to write a paper and she's trying to prove her annoying professor wrong, and to succeed in the academic way that she wants to with her thesis and all those things. But I think in the end that's not really what's driving her. What's driving her is some sort of thrill-seeking thing in the end – she wants to kind of confront something and I think that in the end what she wants to confront is really something that's inside herself in that the only logical explanation for the film is that she committed the murders. (ibid.)

The notion of abjection is one often attached to horror films, particularly to the women characters within them. Barbara Creed (1986) described the horror film as a form of modern defilement rite, by which the woman is subjugated to the Symbolic Order and stripped of her maternal authority. Little has been written, however, on the effect that enacting such rites may have on the actresses themselves, which, despite being 'make-belief' may involve potential humiliation in front of a camera: abuse, mistreatment in terms of nudity, depictions of rape and blood-soaking. One thinks, for example, of Tippi Hedren's traumatic filming of Hitchcock's *The Birds* (1963) in which the actress was scratched and pecked by live birds in the name of film art. Of course, such enactments for the screen may sometimes function as psychotherapy for the people involved, as it seems to have for Madsen during the filming of *Candyman*, the trauma of which led to personal revelation for the actress. In her very candid commentary for the *Candyman* Collector's Edition DVD, Madsen reveals details about her personal life that reflect her role as Helen, and her own marriage at the time:

At first I was a little bit nervous, a bit scared. I was pretty sure that Bernard would take care of me but then again, Bernard's a bit mad, and I thought, I don't know, he's going to really make me do all these insane things, and this was a long shoot, and the movie sort of got darker and darker, and we all got more and more exhausted and it was like, Bernard running around, twirling his hair going 'more blood, more blood, more blood'. And he was just fascinated by this, and every day there was more blood and it was getting to be around the holidays and everyone was really tired, and there was blood everywhere, and every day there was somebody screaming and somebody getting disembowelled… and I think we took about a week off because it just got bad. We all had to walk away for the holidays. We finished on Christmas Eve and we came back right after New Year's because everyone just needed to walk away. That was the only time – it was about a two week period – where it just got very bad. One act-out as to how into this film I was, was towards the middle. We were working these very long hours… and I called home. My then-husband informed me that tonight there would be eight for dinner which was then my cue to become Laura Petrie, and I would stop at the grocery store on the way home to do the shopping, and so I went into this grocery store, it was already night, and as I'm in the check-out line, I'm putting my things down and I'm noticing that the girl is staring at me and she goes, 'excuse me but are you ok?' and I go 'yeah, sure, I'm fine'. And then I realised that I had all this dried fake blood all over my hands, I'd washed, like, really quickly, but I was tired, I had to get to the grocery store before it closed. And then I realised that, it was after the Candyman had sort of cut me with his hook, and I had this long scar and all this blood running down my neck which was now all dry and caked on and in my hair and was sort of smeared down here. And I'd completely forgot, I was so exhausted and so tired, and I knew I couldn't get it off until I was home and in the shower anyway but I'd completely forgotten, so I'd really scared that girl, because I was, like, 'yeah, I'm fine. Whaddya mean? Oh. This is a movie.' That's what I said, 'This is a movie.' And she went, 'ok.' And I just laughed and went home. Poor girl. (*Candyman* DVD commentary, Collector's Edition, 2005)

The 'poor girl' in the scenario perhaps being Madsen herself: expected, as she was, to play the supportive wife whilst at the same time in her role as Helen undergoing hypnosis for the camera, being covered in live bees and fake blood, strip searched, and burnt alive.

FILMING

The sometimes difficult production of *Candyman* as described by Madsen also included two to three days location work in the real Cabrini-Green where Rose filmed exterior, hallway and stairwell scenes. According to Alan Poul, prior to *Candyman* 'no film had ever been shot in some of the tightly gang-controlled sections of Cabrini' (Schwarz, 2004b). Location filming at Cabrini-Green took place outside now demolished apartment buildings at West Walton Street, just west of North Orleans Street, and exteriors of the public toilet where Helen is assaulted in the film were filmed in the

Bernard Rose, Tony Todd and Virginia Madsen on the set of Candyman

south-west corner of North Orleans Street and West Walton Street. Inclusion of these mainly establishing shots creates a sense of realism in the Cabrini-Green sequences, but inevitably involved an element of danger for the actors and film crew.

The producers worked closely with the residents' association and employed Cabrini-Green youths to act in the film, which also served to help the production's credibility with the residents. Clive Barker admits that there were some challenges with the local gangs, 'making sure they were on our side' (Schwarz, 2004b), but with the production providing employment at the projects, filming generally went smoothly. The only major incident happened on the last day when, according to Alan Poul, 'somebody from the roof put a bullet into the camera truck' (ibid.). A number of the film's personnel (some of whom were local Chicagoans who had never been to Cabrini-Green because they were afraid to go there) described how their actual experiences at Cabrini-Green challenged their expectations of the place and its residents. Actor and director Kasi Lemmons (who plays Helen's friend and fellow 'post-structuralist graduate student' Bernadette) remarks on the DVD commentary:

> Cabrini-Green is particularly notorious, and you don't know from what you see in newsflashes or from what you hear, what you are going to find. But we found families.

People just trying to survive. People with nice apartments. Some better than others. And little kids, you know, beautiful little children.

For Todd, however, spending time in Cabrini-Green as part of the film crew raised some difficult emotions, including indignation and guilt:

I tried to come there with no expectations, but I still felt fear. Anybody who didn't belong there was subject to danger. The cops told me to keep my eyes on the rooftops for snipers, and then I ran into a black woman and her two children. They were hustling back from the grocery store before it got dark, and thought the film security people were cops. She asked us when we were going to clean the projects up, which really got to me. (DVD commentary, 2004)

Providing stark contrast to the Cabrini-Green buildings is Helen's International Style apartment building at 957 south-east corner of North Lasalle Street and West Schiller Street, between Old Town and the Gold Coast; and the giant amphitheatre at the University of Illinois photographed from a high angle by helicopter. Most interiors were filmed on sound stages at Occidental Studios in Los Angeles, including the Candyman's lair and the scenes in Helen's apartment; here the film's relatively low budget becomes evident, as Clive Barker has commented on the DVD ('the stuff which is on stage, the interiors, don't look too real to me, unfortunately'). In a sense, the slightly theatrical-looking interiors work with the film's theme of reality blurring into fantasy, and for that reason do not jar with the viewer as they otherwise might have.

SOUNDTRACK

The film's ethereal mood, which counterpoints its gritty setting, fundamental to both 'The Forbidden' and Candyman, is underlined by Philip Glass' celebrated score. The minimalism of Glass' compositions lends Candyman both a feeling of modernity (especially combined with shots of the city's architecture in the film's title sequence) and a sense of the sublime. Bernard Rose had admired Glass before Candyman, and had been particularly impressed by the combination of Glass' score and the travelling aerial views looking down at skyscrapers in Godfrey Reggio's 1982 experimental feature Koyaanisqatsi (which also includes shots of housing projects in disrepair and sequences showing the demolition of a St. Louis housing project). Rose felt that music by Glass would suit his intended title sequence (which features helicopter shots of the Chicago freeway and downtown); but he also wanted a score that would not 'behave in the way that it normally does in a horror movie. Normally the score in a horror movie tells you when you're supposed to be scared, which, to me, is the same thing as telling me I'm not going to be scared' (Schwarz, 2004b). Instead Glass' score functions at a psychological level, and Rose uses sound effects rather than music to help create the jump scares.

Collaborating with Glass meant a different approach to the way that film composers and directors usually work together (whereby the director and the composer go through the film, 'spotting' sequences that require musical accompaniment, and the composer writes only for those specific cues). Glass saw an early assembly of the film and wrote a suite of themes for organ, piano and voice based on his impressions of the film; these incorporated his well-established techniques of 'rhythmic intensity and switching between major and minor key harmonies' (Christensen, 2001). Rose and his editor, Dan Rae, cut the film to the pre-existing demo tracks recorded by Glass, a working practice that enables greater synthesis between image and sound. When the edit was finalised and the picture 'locked', Kurt Munkacsi and Michael Riesman, the producer and conductor of Glass' recordings, orchestrated the cues and recorded them with full choir.

Philip Glass subsequently became embarrassed by the film's success, and removed the score from his CV. According to Don Christensen, who produced the soundtrack to *Candyman: Farewell to the Flesh*, which was built from the original *Candyman* cues:

> The final version of the film was a disappointment to Glass. He felt that he had been manipulated. What was presented to him as a low budget independent project with creative integrity indeed became a low budget Hollywood slasher flick. (2001b)

Christensen's claim (in liner notes accompanying *Candyman*'s eventual release as a soundtrack CD in 2001) that 'somewhere down the line the film's producers and Clive Barker became dissatisfied with Rose's work, probably because he wasn't creating enough overt gore and horror and relieved him of the job of finishing the film' (ibid.) is unfounded (and possibly designed to save face following the decision to release the soundtrack in 2001). It is likely that Glass had become concerned that a score for a horror movie would damage his reputation as one of the world's foremost composers.

However, the soundtrack subsequently found critical acclaim and popularity with fans of Glass, and *Candyman* is now included in the official Philip Glass catalogue of recordings and is available on his label, Orange Mountain Music. (Glass and Bernard Rose would also work together on *Mr. Nice*.)

MPAA RATING

Candyman was submitted to the MPAA who initially awarded an NC-17 rating, mainly due to the special make up-effects in the scene where the Candyman kills the psychiatrist, Dr. Burke. Given the climate at the time, it was inevitable that *Candyman* would face some censorship in order to achieve the preferred 'R' rating (which allows cinema admission to people under the age of 17 accompanied by an adult). In 1992, the NC-17 rating was new (having replaced the 'X' in 1990) and still carried some of the stigma of an 'adults only' categorisation; some newspapers refused to run ads for NC-17 films and a number of video stores declined to carry those titles. *Candyman*'s distributor Columbia/TriStar opted to resubmit the film for cuts; the MPAA asked for excisions to the psychiatrist's murder scene: to lessen the blood spray after the Candyman's hook emerges from the man's stomach, and to reduce the man's screams and his violent shaking. Columbia/TriStar agreed to these cuts in order to secure an 'R' for the film. In the US the 'R' version was released on VHS in the 1990s, and on DVD in 2001. In the UK (according to the BBFC at http://www.bbfc.co.uk/releases/candyman-1992) all known versions of *Candyman* have been 'passed uncut'; it is possible that the film's original UK distributor, Rank Film Ltd., submitted the 'R' version to the BBFC. However, in the UK, Channel 4 has been known to show the uncut 'NC-17' version of the film.

US THEATRICAL RELEASE

Candyman's world premiere took place at the 1992 Toronto Film Festival, playing as part of the Midnight Madness line-up (which also included the Belgian black comedy *Man Bites Dog* [1992] and Peter Jackson's splatstick classic *Braindead* [1992]) in September that year. The film's theatrical release came at a time of great racial tension in Los Angeles. According to Bernard Rose, *Candyman* had a test screening scheduled on the day that the Rodney King riots broke out; this would mark the screening as taking place in April 1992, several months before *Candyman*'s US theatrical release in October. Perhaps because of the riots, some LA newspaper critics received the film with hostility; most notably the *Los Angeles Times* critic, Kevin Thomas, who described *Candyman* as 'pretentious and preposterous'. In other cities, it was more favourably received. Janet Maslin of the *New York Times*, praised Madsen's performance, Rose's direction and the cinematography of Anthony B. Richmond, and noted the film's 'unusually high interest in social issues'. Roger Ebert, as we know, praised the film highly; as did *Variety*, whose staff film critic called it 'an upper-register horror item that delivers the requisite shocks and gore but doesn't cheat or cop out'.

As Clive Barker has remarked in his DVD commentary, there was genuine fear amongst the movie executives that, in the aftermath of the riots, the film would be seen as racist: 'that we were going to have mass demonstrations and fist fights and worse at the cinemas where the thing was showing'. However, as the film's opening weekend proved, inner city audiences took to *Candyman* immediately. Bernard Rose confirms: 'urban audiences… from the get-go liked the movie. Rather than regarding [a black monster] as any kind of detriment it was helping the movie play' (Schwarz, 2004b).

In its opening weekend *Candyman* took $5,404,320 and went on to gross $25,792,310 at the US box office, playing 1500 theatres (*Box Office Mojo*). As Poul comments on the DVD track, this was a significant financial return for a horror film at that time. Moreover, the film was a success on home video (*Candyman* was financed on a video deal with Columbia/TriStar) and cable, where its fan base has increased year on year. *Candyman* is currently ranked 34 in Horror-Slashers (*Box Office Mojo*) based on its life-time gross (and number 1 in the Clive Barker brand – ahead of *Hellraiser*). According to IMDb users, *Candyman*'s biggest fans are men and women aged 30-44, many of whom have grown up with the film; and it is also popular with viewers aged 18-29, suggesting that it has appeal to younger horror fans. A typical user review on IMDb ('Steevh' from Hastings, England) begins:

> Deeply disturbing, intelligently made and without a screaming teen in sight, *Candyman* is one of the stand-out horror movies of the decade. (http://www.imdb.com/title/ tt0103919/reviews)

4. CANDYMAN AND THE RETURN OF THE REPRESSED

In 1979, Robin Wood, drawing on the writings of Herbert Marcuse (by way of Gad Horowitz), proposed that 'the true subject of the horror genre is the struggle for recognition of all that our civilisation represses or oppresses' (2003:68). The monster symbolises a return of the repressed in the form of the Other which poses a threat to the dominant order. Wood regarded the horror film as a potentially progressive genre insomuch as the dread of social, sexual and ideological difference is challenged when the Other is rendered sympathetic and understandable to the viewer and thereby cannot be recuperated into dominant ideology. (If we go by Wikipedia, 'recuperation', in the sociological sense, is 'the process by which politically radical ideas and images are twisted, co-opted, absorbed, defused, incorporated, annexed and commodified within media culture and bourgeois society, and thus become interpreted through a neutralized, innocuous or more socially conventional perspective. More broadly, it may refer to the cultural appropriation of any subversive works or ideas by mainstream culture.')

As Kirsten Moana Thompson remarks, the Candyman is the return of the repressed as 'national allegory': he is a supernatural being who re-enacts his own physical torture on the bodies of his victims. In this way, 'the historical trauma of white violence against African-Americans is displaced onto the supernatural formation and circulation of the legend of Candyman, and is signalled by the dread that his legend prompts' (2007: 65). That the Candyman is, in Rose's words, 'a representative of people who are oppressed', lends him an element of sympathy.

A number of critics have commented on the reactionary nature of the horror genre in the 1980s and 1990s. For Robin Wood this is symptomatic of a tradition that has always existed in the genre and which becomes dominant under certain social conditions (2003: 170). The era of Margaret Thatcher and Ronald Reagan instituted a neoconservative agenda; a return to family values and a move against liberalism. This was reflected in horror cinema entering a deeply conservative phase in the late 1970s and early/mid-1980s (as can be seen in the slasher cycle [1979-1983] that dominated the genre during that period). At that time a radical horror cinema of the type that had emerged with *Night of the Living Dead* (1968) seemed untenable: the key directors of the '70s – George A. Romero, Wes Craven, David Cronenberg, John Carpenter, Jeff Lieberman – went mainstream, left the genre altogether or fell silent. It was only with the rise of body horror and splatstick in the late '80s/early '90s that a new generation of independent film-makers such as Frank Henenlotter, Sam Raimi, Stuart Gordon, Peter Jackson and Brian Yuzna rediscovered the genre's capacity for social transgression. However, these filmmakers worked with low budgets for the direct-to-video market, and for the most part their films received little or no exposure theatrically. The genre became marginalised.

By the '90s mainstream horror had mutated into the more culturally acceptable psychological thriller (*The Silence of the Lambs* [1991]) or the pastiche horror (*Bram Stoker's Dracula* [1992]; *Scream* [1996]). Some critics have argued that whilst '80s and '90s horror movies are affected by conservative values, they are not entirely to be neglected. Tony Williams contends that family values in these films are not always victorious, and that works of the '80s and '90s, although not oppositional, show a hesitancy to affirm dominant values (2015: 205). However, others have asserted that the postmodern or neoconservative horror film – of which *Candyman* is often cited as an example – offers a dominant order that is simultaneously discredited and affirmed.

Christopher Sharrett asserts that neoconservative culture is necessarily concerned with the restoration of the Other. As the horror film addresses the Other at the primal level of the unconscious, the project of the neoconservative horror film is to overturn, or co-opt, horror's radicalism (2015: 282-283). It is the inherent contradiction of neoconservative culture that dominant ideology allows for depictions of its own destruction but will not permit the envisaging of a political alternative to capitalism. There exists in the dominant culture, as Wood remarks, a taboo on imagining alternatives to a system that 'can be exposed as monstrous, oppressive, and unworkable but which must nevertheless not be *constructively* challenged' (2003: 142, emphasis in original). In the horror film, this often translates as showing society in breakdown whilst stopping short of actually presenting any way out of apocalypse. As part of capitalism's re-legitimation, the neoconservative horror film, according to Sharrett, 'necessarily reinstitutes gender, class, and racial polarization and subjugation while allowing and even advancing discourses that reveal the bankruptcy of such manifestations of capitalist society' (2015: 283). In other words, the postmodern/neoconservative horror film may appear to take a subversive perspective on difference, but ultimately seeks to reinforce traditional prejudices and phobias. A number of critics have levelled this accusation at *Candyman*.

In one of the earliest critical pieces to appear on the film, Antonis Balasopoulos makes the point that *Candyman*'s overt connection between blackness and monstrosity can be seen as an indication of the '90s horror film's shift towards 'a more conservative and even reactionary ideology'; and in that sense seems to reverse the racial politics of the horror movies of the late 1960s and early 1970s in a way that would place it within the category of neoconservative horror text (1997: 30). Balasopoulos, however, goes on to question clean-cut oppositions between 1960s/1970s progressiveness and 1980s/1990s reactionary conservatism, and suggests that *Candyman* develops a more complex and contradictory problematic around questions of difference, one that 'spins around and spills over axes of race, gender, and class in modern-day urban America' (ibid.)

In his recent book, *Twenty-First Century Horror Films*, Douglas Keesey remarks that the most intriguing horror films may be the ones in which 'the characters (and the filmmakers) are trying to work out how they feel about "others", questioning received notions – and genre conventions – regarding what is threatening or "monstrous", and seeking out new perspectives beyond a dread of difference' (2017: 13). He concludes that most horror films involve 'some combination' of the progressive and the regressive (ibid.). Wood has himself remarked of the horror film, 'the genre carries within itself the capability of reactionary inflection' and perhaps no horror film (no matter how progressive in its potential) is 'entirely immune from its operations' (2003:170).

Candyman, in adopting the return of the repressed schema, whilst remaining a neoconservative horror film, can, in this way, be seen to combine the progressive and the regressive in an ambiguous manner that Gad Horowitz would term 'duplicitous': in other words, as a cultural work, *Candyman* might be read as *simultaneously* progressive and regressive, as will be explored in the analysis that follows.

CANDYMAN – ANALYSIS

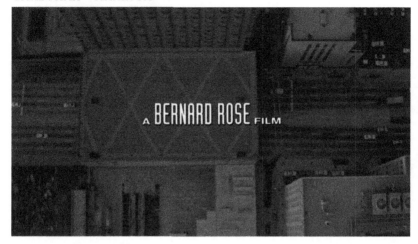

Candyman's *credits sequence*

The opening titles of *Candyman*, whilst consciously inspired by Hitchcock's *North by Northwest* (1959), serve to present the idea of Urban Gothic. The use of the Philip Glass score over these helicopter shots of downtown Chicago, as Stacey Abbott observes, 'inscribes the City with a Gothic sensibility' that will be reinforced later: the combination of image and sound evoke a 'monstrous history of this urban space' (2015: 69-78). Already we are given the sense of social divisions through geographic areas. The camera swoops over a tunnel, crosses a river. (A man's voice is heard briefly, indistinctly, like a muffled snippet from a radio news broadcast.) A feeling of dislocation is emphasised by the Saul Bass-like title graphics themselves, which bisect the image. They move together and then drift apart, like the Chicago highways that converge and diverge demarcating the city's socio-economic sectors.

We cut to a mass of bees, 'dimly perceived, packed together, crawling over one another' (Rose, 1991:1), an allusion perhaps to the inhabitants of the city, and a link to the historical trauma of America's colonial past. In the nineteenth century, as Thompson notes, Chicago was an industrial/transportation centre and principal site of immigration for blacks fleeing slavery (2007: 67). The Candyman's vengeful spirit remains, demanding retribution for past (and present) injustices, manifest in the bees that stung him to death.

We hear his intonation: 'They will say that I have shed innocent blood. What's blood for, if not for shedding?' We zoom in slowly to the swarming mass as the Candyman informs us, 'With my hook for a hand, I'll split you from your gullet to your groin'. The bees rise as a vast cloud over the cityscape, a symbol of the 'blot' that America's racial history casts over the modern metropolis. As Lola Landekic has written of this sequence:

> The haunting of places is a horror standard, but *Candyman* takes it further, positing the city itself as a malevolent force, swallowing the main characters. What happens when an urban centre is built on top of terrible trauma? Where does that energy go? One need only look at a city's marginalized peoples and its housing projects, the 'dangerous' zones, to understand the legacy of colonialism. All so-called 'bad neighbourhoods' are places haunted by trauma, and word of mouth ensures the patterns are maintained.
> (*Art of the Title*, 2016)

Downtown Chicago obliterated by bees

The dissolve from the wide shot of downtown Chicago obliterated by bees to a striking close-up of Helen is already in the screenplay, an indication of the thematic importance of this segue from the 'mini-overture' of the title sequence to the story proper. Rose describes the transition in the screenplay thus: 'the bees appear to float across her fine features through the dissolve' (1991: 1). Already Helen, as a woman, is linked to the Candyman as a representative of 'people who are oppressed'. This is reinforced

The Chicago landscape dissolves to a close-up of Helen (Virginia Madsen)

by the words, 'I came for you', spoken by the Candyman over the dissolve, and by the *Candyman* theme playing on a music box as the diegetic score.

As I remarked in my introduction, this is to be Helen's story ultimately. She is already in a liminal state at the start of the film and what Helen really sees in the mirror as she summons the Candyman later on is a premonition of what she will become, an early recognition of her dispossessed 'Other' self. *Candyman* is structured around Helen's journey towards this realisation and, in the end, towards her state of transcendence.

'THIS IS THE SCARIEST STORY I EVER HEARD AND IT'S TOTALLY TRUE'

Helen's starting point is her research project, ostensibly into urban legend, but more generally into social 'truth' behind urban myth. The first version of the Candyman urban legend we see is, as Thompson points out, an allusion to the slasher horror film of the early 1980s (2007: 61). Rose films the sequence (which essentially retells the babysitter legend) like a cheap '80s horror, setting it in a *Halloween* house in a white suburb where a homicidal maniac threatens sexually active teenagers.

We might see this episode as commentary both on the urban legend 'rule' that transgression must trigger some form of punishment and the reactionary nature of the '80s slasher itself in which sexual activity leads to death. Thereby the urban myth is initially associated with a moral conservatism concerning youth sexuality originating in the '50s but still evident in the '80s and continuing into the era of *Candyman*. Sexual repression is therefore the first 'return' to be explored in the film through the examination of urban myth and its influence on horror cinema. (It is worth noting that Brian De Palma does something similar in the opening scene of *Blow Out* [1981], which presents a 'film-within-a-film' [a spoof '80s slasher called 'Co-ed Frenzy'] as a commentary on the misogyny of the slasher cycle.)

A dissolve returns us to the diegetic story, and we are introduced fully to Helen. Rose emphasises her sense of superiority over the freshmen that she interviews ('seems like they are getting younger every day'). As Andrea Kuhn notes, the first part of the film follows 'Helen's illusion of being firmly rooted in the Symbolic… she expresses her assumed superiority in her knowing smile, the ironic and teasing comments towards her (black) partner, her privileged social position and her self-assessment as an explorer finding "truth", where others are scared off by superstition and fear'. But, as Kuhn points out, Helen's status 'remains severely compromised by her gender. As a woman she is constantly marginalized by the men surrounding her. The array of male authorities in *Candyman* deny her access to power, privilege and security' (2000).

Rose establishes a sense of institutionalised misogyny in the scenes that follow. We see Helen from overhead, dwarfed by more architecture: the University's giant amphitheatre, a symbol of educational tradition. Trevor, her 'dullard' (Schwarz, 2004b) husband, is afforded the seat of learning; and commands a lecture theatre, whereas Helen must content herself for the time being with a place at the back of the class.

Behind Trevor on a chalkboard are written the essential elements of urban legends – and indeed of the film's narrative – 'a victim seeking revenge…resides in a "forbidden area"…Deformities…appliances (blades, hooks)'. Trevor glibly holds forth with his students, and we see Helen's dismayed reaction to his inadequate conclusion that urban myths are no more than 'the unselfconscious reflection of the fears of society'. We sense Helen's dissatisfaction with Trevor's explanation, her desire to go beyond the commonplace, to break boundaries. Trevor's lecture may broach the 'problem', but it evades the question of repression/oppression and its inexorable return.

Helen's gaze is fixed on Stacey (Carolyn Lowery), who will become Trevor's mistress, and already Helen feels a sense of threat: that she will be replaced by someone younger and more servile than herself. It is revealed that Helen is also angry because Trevor has delivered the urban legend lecture before Helen has finished gathering her data from the freshmen. Trevor has, as Kuhn points out, ruined her plans to carry out an important survey for her thesis, a deliberate attempt to undermine her academic career and to compromise her status in order to boost his own (2000). Helen's angry look as Trevor exits the scene reveals her resentment.

'I AM THE WRITING ON THE WALL, THE WHISPER IN THE CLASSROOM'

The film moves directly from the division of male/female power to the division of race and class. We see Helen working alone, transcribing her interviews; Henrietta (Barbara Alston), a black female cleaner, becomes visible in the background of the shot, belittled in the frame, denoting her status as a menial. Kim D. Hester-Williams makes the point that *Candyman* represents a desire to appropriate racially coded difference in order to 'reconcile the longing for an American subjectivity that finds itself in a constant state of becoming rather than being'. The promise of America, a promise based on the dream of freedom, remains a work in progress, and existing alongside that dream, according to Hester-Williams, has always been the 'concomitant nightmare of slavery' (2004: 1). When the subject of the Candyman is broached, Henrietta displays the 'remove' characteristic of urban myth retelling: *she* doesn't live in the projects but her friend does (although Trevor's blackboard tells us that the Southside, too, is where urban myths originate, linked as they are in *Candyman* to urban poverty).

Even though the camera remains on or close to Helen throughout the film, establishing subjectivity (it becomes clear early on that we are to experience from her vantage point the urban legend), Rose allows a brief cut away at this point to the two black women – Kitty (Sarina Grant), Henrietta's friend and co-worker, lives further down the poverty line in Cabrini-Green – before returning to Helen's reaction as she is told about the murder of Ruthie-Jean. This subjectivity is itself potentially problematic, as the site of oppression is subtly moved away from the black women to the white liberal protagonist; and from there, it becomes possible to argue that *Candyman*, as a neoconservative horror film, represents white liberal co-optation of black experience. However, part of the film's fascination resides in the tension created by this struggle for subjectivity by the various social groups in the film: Helen, the white male academics, the Cabrini-Green gangs, Jake, the police, Dr. Burke, Anne-Marie, and of course, the Candyman himself, all attempt to seize the meaning of the narrative for themselves.

Candyman might, in other words, be taken (in relation to Rose's later *Frankenstein*), as a meditation on the workings of a society based on the strict divisions of immense wealth and squalid poverty where rank and status are stratified by subdivisions of race, gender and class, and where a struggle for power and recognition amongst these social groupings becomes inevitable. This is in fact underlined in the very next scene in which Helen examines a microfilm of Ruthie-Jean's murder as reported by the newspapers. We see a headline: WHAT KILLED RUTHIE-JEAN? LIFE IN THE PROJECTS.

Indeed, *Candyman*'s unity as a horror film is achieved by Rose's seamless merging of cinematic influences into a coherent whole. As well as referencing '80s slashers, *Candyman* draws heavily on such films as *Repulsion* (1965) and, as in this short scene, *The Exorcist* (1973). Here the mundane material world of microfiche readers, cassette recorders, university buildings – the rational world – contrasts with the uncanny. Helen, like Damian Karras (Jason Miller) in *The Exorcist*, is an investigator traversing the boundaries of the rational and the supernatural. It is this liminality that draws Helen to the Candyman.

'AN ENTIRE COMMUNITY STARTS ATTRIBUTING THE DAILY HORRORS OF THEIR LIVES TO A MYTHICAL FIGURE'

An establishing shot of Helen's apartment; before that, the camera cranes away from a park – behind it are what we take to be the towers of Cabrini-Green in the distance – emphasising both the proximity and the divide of the upmarket neighbourhood and the projects. The scene that follows is about the connection between Helen's apartment and Cabrini-Green, between Helen and the Candyman. (What attracts Helen to the mystery of the Candyman may indeed be a nascent sense of her own marginalisation/oppression.) Indeed, Helen's apartment building is here revealed to have been originally built as a housing project; however, as Helen explains to Bernadette, 'the city soon realised there was no barrier between here and the Gold Coast'. As previously mentioned, Linda Williams has identified that there exists in horror films 'a surprising (and at times subversive) affinity between monster and woman, the sense in which her look at the monster recognises their similar status within patriarchal structures of seeing' (1984: 62). It is this affinity between monster and woman that lies at the heart of *Candyman*. As Williams points out, the strange sympathy that often develops between the monster and the girl 'may be less an expression of sexual desire and more a flash of sympathetic identification' (ibid.). And so it is between Helen and the Candyman.

Lucy Donaldson observes the way *Candyman* emphasises the connectedness of the Candyman and Helen, of monster and victim, who are both 'ambiguously embodied, becoming more like doubles than clearly defined binary figures' (2011: 32). In the Gothic, as Donaldson notes, the double is a device which allows a character to 'perceive more clearly and personally both worlds and both sides of his or her self' (ibid.). The mirror in Helen's bathroom that links apartments in her building complex (an actual detail of the Chicago housing projects which Rose incorporated into the story) metaphorically links Helen's apartment to Cabrini-Green and Helen to the Candyman.

As Helen and Bernadette remove the mirror to expose an opening into the next apartment, we cut to their point of view of the adjacent empty bathroom. The camera slowly zooms in, emphasising the dead space, creating a sense of unease. The vacant apartment becomes a 'forbidden' place, and, as we know from Trevor's blackboard, 'the victim seeking revenge resides in a forbidden area'. Transgressing a forbidden area, be it a geographical trespass, or a moral transgression, is, as previously mentioned, a trigger for retribution in urban myth and folk tales. The forbidden or bloody chamber motif dates back to the Bluebeard legend: a nobleman forbids his new bride from entering a chamber in his castle; unbeknownst to her, this is where he keeps the bodies of his previous wives whom he has murdered. In the story, the curious girl transgresses this directive and narrowly avoids the same fate as the other women. *Candyman* plays on

Bernadette Walsh (Kasi Lemmons) and Helen (Virginia Madsen) attempt to look beyond the mirror

our expectations arising from such patriarchal fairy stories in which women's curiosity is punished by dire consequences.

Indeed, Helen and Bernadette are aware of their transgression and giggle like teenagers as they recite the Candyman incantation. However, only Helen can bring herself to say the final chant which will complete the invocation, and as she does so – significantly – she leans in closer to the mirror as if peering into herself. Helen's curiosity may not in fact arise from a childish or childlike desire to transgress; rather it is her wish to perceive more clearly both worlds and both sides of herself that seems to make her cross the boundary into the Candyman's realm.

Laura Wyrick comments that on a basic psychoanalytic level, Helen's staring into the mirror to summon the Candyman 'indicates that Candyman dwells in the desiring subject's unconsciousness'. It also indicates the paradox, according to Wyrick, that, underlying Lacan's conception of the mirror stage of a child's development, 'creating a unified self necessitates recognising a split self, and that the created self is never alone but always already under an/Other's gaze' (1998: 95). For a child, the mirror stage is anticipatory: a first step into the 'masculine' world of order and authority that we inhabit as adults, the Symbolic real of pre-established language systems which, according to

Lacan, oppresses women in the 'Name of the Father'. For an adult to repeat this stage
(as Helen appears to) 'indicates a return to an already temporally disruptive action,
a double move that takes on the inverse structure of reflection' (Wyrick, 1998: 95).
In both cases, according to Wyrick, 'the mirror establishes a liminal space where the
individual and the social meet to construct and disprove each other'. Helen is ostensibly
an adult, but she is treated like a child by the academic establishment, including Trevor,
and the film connects her with children and childishness (her rescue of the stolen baby,
Anthony, is particularly significant in this respect). Therefore her repetitions of the mirror
stage invoke a 'narcissistic nostalgia for an originary unity' and an uncanny recognition
of an 'alienating identity' that will later be assumed. As Wyrick observes, this alienating
identity is the Candyman: 'at once self and Other, at once subject and object of Helen's
reflection' (ibid.).

Rose segues via a sound bridge into Helen's bathroom later that night. The camera
tracks back from the mirror into the apartment, evoking an unseen presence that might
be a direct result of the earlier invocation of the Candyman. This is a play on generic
expectation leading to a jump scare (the first of many in the film). The use of silence
(punctuated only by a ticking clock – another nod to *Repulsion*) helps to build this sense
of anticipation and unease. The camera finds Helen asleep in bed. There is a crucifix
hanging on the wall above her, the only reference in the film to Helen and/or Trevor's
religious beliefs. It is also another early indication of the film's supernatural element
(it may also signify Helen's need to 'believe'). There is a Val Lewton-type 'bus' moment
as Trevor enters the frame suddenly; he is, however, not the Candyman, and so our
expectations on another level are not yet fulfilled. Helen has not at this point crossed
the threshold from the rational world into the uncanny one.

'WHITE PEOPLE NEVER COME 'ROUND HERE EXCEPT TO CAUSE US A PROBLEM'

Indeed, the liminal moment comes in the next sequence, and, in 1992, was to be all
the more unexpected for the reason that the uncanny space in *Candyman* is also an
urban one. Stacey Abbott notes that *Candyman* immerses the audience 'within a Gothic
understanding of the modern city, both real and mythic' (2015: 69). As Helen and

Bernadette drive to Cabrini-Green we are given the sense of them crossing a threshold leading into the Gothic. Here Rose plays on the irrational fear of the projects, presenting them as the contemporary equivalent of the haunted house. Bernadette carries an arsenal of self-defence products with her. 'What do you think's going to happen?' Helen asks incredulously. 'They're going to shoot you? Rape you?' From this irrational fear of the 'wrong part of town', it becomes possible for the film to move seamlessly into the Gothic. The gangbangers patrolling Cabrini-Green are threshold guardians, there to ensure that Helen, as the protagonist, is worthy of crossing into the uncanny space of Cabrini-Green. Initially, they bar the entrance, and Helen (and Bernadette) are forced to muster their courage and determination in order to cross into the Gothic realm.

Rose utilises the Steadicam in such a way that the viewer is led across the boundary with them. The line between documentary reality and the Gothic is further blurred by the film's use of the actual Cabrini-Green location. How much of the graffiti, for example, is genuine and how much a construct of the art department? As they move from the stairwells into the corridors of the complex, we change from the real location to a set, but again the transition is subliminal. 'Sweets to the Sweet' is scrawled on the wall of a corridor; another indication of the move into the uncanny, as this, we can surmise, is the work of the Candyman. The message is ostensibly for Helen herself: she is 'the sweet', the object of the Candyman's affection. In Barker's story, Helen's surname is Buchanan; but Rose changes it to 'Lyle' in the film, a probable reference to Tate and Lyle, the British sugar-refining business and manufacturer of Lyle's Golden Syrup. According to Barker:

> I use a quote from Hamlet in that story: Sweets to the Sweet. In England we have Golden Syrup. The makers of this syrup put on their can a partially rotted corpse of a lion with bees flying around it. The quote that's at the bottom is 'from the strong shall come sweetness'. ('And he said unto them, Out of the eater came forth meat, and out of the strong came forth sweetness' – Judges 14:10-14.) I like the idea that there be something perversely sweet about the monstrous. (Schwarz, 2004b)

Rose makes an explicit reference to that image later in the film, when the Candyman opens his chest cavity and the bees fly out.

Bernadette (Kasi Lemmons) and Helen (Virginia Madsen) in Cabrini-Green

We are given another jump scare in the first Cabrini-Green sequence as Anne-Marie appears with a Rottweiler (she too functions as a threshold guardian here). Helen and Bernadette approach what might be thought of as the film's main forbidden chamber or innermost cave: the derelict apartment, site of Ruthie-Jean's murder, the inside of which the Candyman has made his lair. 'The layout is identical,' the characters note; again, this resemblance of the two apartments in Cabrini-Green and Helen's building emphasises the connection between Helen and the Candyman, and their seemingly disparate worlds existing in parallel (geographically and psychically the two realms will eventually collapse into one). As they enter Ruthie-Jean's apartment, Bernadette is still the more cautious of the two; Helen the more determined. In the squalid bathroom, there is another mirror, which here functions as a liminal space: 'this is where he crawled through', we are told.

The camera again moves into a forbidden space: that of the Candyman's lair. As Helen enters 'through the mirror', the lighting on her emphasises the crossing from 'reality' to the realm of the Romantic sublime. It is significant that Helen makes this journey alone, without Bernadette. Their separation is emphasised by the cross-cutting. The black woman is here marginalised in the narrative.

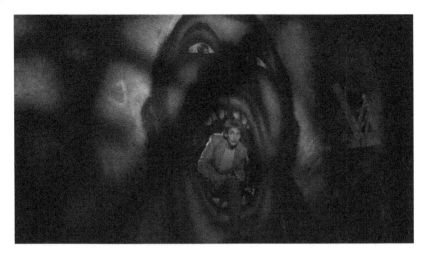

Through the mouth of his mural, Helen (Virginia Madsen) enters the Candyman's lair

Edmund Burke's 'Philosophical Enquiry', written in 1757, connected the sublime with experiences of awe, terror and danger; Rose brilliantly evokes the sublime in the next shot, when a slow zoom-out reveals the Candyman's mural. Is it significant that Helen, like the bees, emerges from his mouth? The camera frames a close-up of the eyes of the mural from Helen's point of view (described in the screenplay thus: 'somewhere in his eyes is a melancholy'). This is an image that will be repeated several times, at key moments throughout the film, in near-subliminal flash frames. Helen is already semi-hypnotised, under the Candyman's influence. It is here in this scene that Candyman is linked to real urban legends, as Helen discovers candy contaminated by razorblades. These are sweets to the sweet: to Helen from the Candyman. Bernadette, meanwhile, is alone outside the apartment. She discovers a broken, discarded child's doll; another link to childishness (later, Bernadette will be splayed open like a rag doll), and a deflection from the jump scare that follows as Helen suddenly appears at the hole that leads into the apartment. A further *Repulsion*-inspired scare quickly ensues as Bernadette closes the bathroom cabinet and the figure of Anne-Marie is revealed behind them like an apparition (the Candyman later displays the ability to materialise at will).

In the scene that follows, in which Anne-Marie allows the two women into her home, Anne-Marie, like the black cleaners earlier, is at first shown from a distance but then given dignity by the camera. She is represented to have more integrity than Helen at this point, who is opportunistically trying to gain access to the apartment in order to get information from Anne-Marie. Eventually Rose's camera lends Anne-Marie dominance as she berates the two graduate students for seeking to exploit the Cabrini-Green residents with their study. Anne-Marie lowers her defences when Helen helps with her baby, Anthony. This is presented as a point of identification between the two women, although we wonder if Helen's comment that she would 'love to have' a child of her own is sincere, or said merely to gain Anne-Marie's confidence. The child's later rescue from the flames of the bonfire will pave the way for the final stages of Helen's journey towards the creation of a unified self. Hence, Anne-Marie leads Helen closer to the Candyman with her testimony regarding the night of Ruthie-Jean's murder (which Anne-Marie heard through the walls of her apartment). Rose moves the camera in closer as the scene plays out, until Helen and Anne-Marie are framed in matching tight close ups: emphasising the commonality created between them by the Candyman myth.

'THE LEGEND FIRST APPEARED IN 1890. CANDYMAN WAS THE SON OF A SLAVE'

We cut to a close-up of Helen in a restaurant, still haunted by Anne-Marie's story. The scene that follows provides a closer link between Helen's two worlds of academia and Cabrini-Green. Ostensibly the scene is about Helen's learning of the Candyman's backstory: the obese senior academic Philip Purcell (Michael Culkin) delivers oral history of how the Candyman was murdered for his social transgressions; on another level, however, it is about the ranks of academia, the power structure, and Helen's subjugation to the males within the academic world. As Hester-Williams comments, it is in this scene that Helen becomes 'ensnared by both an indirect and direct identification with the white landowner's daughter' of the legend (whom she physically resembles, it is later revealed, and may be a reincarnation of) and 'the horror of nineteenth-century American slavery, as symbolized by the mutilated black body of Candyman' (2004: 4).

Like the Candyman, Helen is initially disempowered, and comes to realise her low status amongst the white males. The scene marks the start of her realisation that, like the poor blacks, she is marginalised because of her difference. Although white and middle-class, as a woman and a junior researcher her position within the academy is a precarious one. Academia (as presented in the film) has a clear hierarchy linked to seniority and reputation (and, it would appear, race, class and gender). In some ways the scene is analogous to the Candyman's background as a painter of portraits for noblemen which made him highly sought after when it came to 'the documenting of one's wealth and position in society'. As the scene progresses, the lighting on Helen changes – it becomes the 'Candyman' lighting – a stylised portraiture that the film adopts for Helen whenever she is in the Candyman's presence. In other words, the scene already suggests that his story is hers. Like the Candyman, Helen will be chased and mutilated as a result of her lower position in society. We flash frame the eyes of the Candyman mural: again we see the hypnotic effect on Helen – her sympathy for his plight.

In cutting to the scene that follows, in which Helen returns to Cabrini-Green, the picture transition precedes the sound transition. It is a way of compressing time, as we move to the next scene visually whilst hearing the last lines of dialogue from the current scene. A common technique in feature films, but here Rose uses it to conflate events; Helen's entry into the Candyman's past, and his origin as an urban myth, combine with her return to Cabrini-Green to photograph the mural.

'I HEAR YOU'RE LOOKING FOR CANDYMAN, BITCH'

Robin Wood listed children amongst his categories of Other, claiming that they may in fact be the most oppressed section of the population: 'the otherness of children is that which is repressed within ourselves, its expression therefore hated in others. What the previous generation repressed in us, we, in turn, repress in our children' (2003: 67). The character of Jake (played by DeJuan Guy) seems set to perpetuate the myth of the Candyman through his belief in the urban legend ('I can't say nothing – or Candyman will get me'). We can only imagine that he is destined to become a member of a gang when he gets older. Significantly, however, Jake is ultimately presented as a force for social change: it is Jake who later leads the residents to burn the Candyman in a bid to end his tyranny over the projects. At first Helen doesn't attempt to dissuade Jake from his belief in the Candyman; instead she uses him to show her where the Candyman 'lives' – she plays on his belief. It is only after she (apparently) solves the mystery of the Candyman that she tells him what she thinks is the truth, and therefore acts responsibly towards the boy. This comes after she has been attacked in the public toilet: her sympathy for Jake at that point relates to the story that he has told her about the 'retarded' boy who is castrated in the toilets, and may be Helen's attempt to relieve Jake of his own castration fears.

Abjection becomes a key motif of *Candyman* from this point in the film. Clive Barker has talked of Julia Kristeva's theory of abjection in terms of taboo and repressed material 'that has been thrown out of the culture, abandoned' but which nevertheless needs 'to go somewhere' as it is 'a part of what it is to be human' (Schwartz, 2004a). Hence the filthy public lavatory (in the screenplay Rose is emphatic about the abject elements of the scene: 'the filth is indescribable') with Sweets to the Sweet 'written in shit' on the walls, and the toilet bowl filled with bees – a surreal, inexplicable moment, but clearly Freudian, as these are also the bees that engulfed Chicago as the spirit of the Candyman. In the lavatory, Helen experiences another flashback to the mural, indicating the Candyman's presence, as though Helen senses that the Candyman is waiting for her in his abject state.

Here also, pseudo-ostension comes into play within the narrative. Outside, Jake waits, and 'a large MAN – we see only his back – steps into frame' (Rose, 1991: 41). Jake calls him 'Candyman', and indeed he does brandish a large hook. Rose has stated that he wanted to stay away from the rape scenario that he sees as being central to many horror films; however that suggestion is present in this scene. Rose alternates long shots showing the exterior – as the gang leave the public restroom – and close-ups of Jake's reaction as he enters to find Helen unconsciousness. The alternation of shot sizes has an almost hypnotic effect on the viewer, as we intersperse points of view between Jake and Helen. However, cutting away from Helen at the point where she is attacked to Jake outside watching the toilet, serves to obscure what might be taking place in the restroom. This suggestion is heightened by the direct cut to a police line-up of a group of black men, amongst whom Helen identifies her attacker. The male gang leader masquerading as the Candyman is one more in a succession of men, who, in the film, deny Helen power, privilege and security, here through violent action.

'CANDYMAN ISN'T REAL. HE'S JUST A STORY'

As Kuhn notes, the law, in the guise of an older (black) police detective protects Helen at first, but finally arrests 'and even institutionalises her, making her the helpless victim of the monster' (2000). However, that subversive plot twist is yet to come. At this point in the story, Rose brilliantly appears to resolve the story in prosaic fashion, with all the mundanity of the average made-for-TV movie. The Candyman attacker is revealed to be nothing more than a hoaxer, a drug overlord who assumed the Candyman persona in order to keep the Cabrini-Green residents in fear. Helen has a scene with Jake in which she debunks the Candyman myth for the child once and for all, symbolising that she is also admitting to herself that the Candyman (and all that he has come to represent to her in the film) does not exist, and therefore any further (self) examination can be dismissed as unnecessary ('now that he's locked up everything's going to be okay'). The psyche is so conditioned into accepting repression as the norm that when liberation or revelation occurs, it is often accompanied by feelings of guilt and a withdrawal back into the repressed state.

Wood typifies the 'happy ending' of the horror film as 'signifying the restoration of repression' (2003: 68). After her assault in the public toilet, Helen appears to have 'learned her lesson' and returned to a state of repression. She is now content to play the good wife to Trevor, preparing meals for him and welcoming him home, no longer questioning his male privilege (which includes turning a blind eye to his philandering). There is a repeat of the shot of the campus amphitheatre, and Helen and Bernadette are reunited with the news that their research is to be published, suggesting their recuperation ('a nice little boring thesis regurgitating all the usual crap about urban legends') as academics. There is even a message of white liberalism to the viewer, with Helen herself as the mouthpiece: 'Two people get murdered, and the cops do nothing. A white woman gets attacked and they lock the place down.' *Candyman* could well have ended there, as a glib comment on the racial, gender and class divisions in America which, despite its liberal platitudes, actually serves to continue normality, 'rationality' and the socio-political status quo. However, Rose has merely tricked us into forming this conclusion in order to move us instead into the supernatural, the irrational and the transgressive.

'YOU WERE NOT CONTENT WITH THE STORIES, SO I WAS OBLIGED TO COME'

Tony Todd's first appearance as the Candyman

At 42 minutes – almost half-way into the film – the Candyman appears. The meeting between Helen and the Candyman takes place in a multi-storey car park: the cinematic 'go-to' for a clandestine meeting. Here, however, Rose emphasises the liminality of the space. The camera moves around Helen as she unlocks her car, to reveal the Candyman in the same frame: no longer myth, he has crossed over into the real world to become a tangible presence, at least to Helen. We flash frame to the Candyman mural and then to a near-subliminal shot of Helen from later in the film, where she 'sees' baby Anthony in the Candyman's lair. The strobe light on her face links also to the brief scene where she is driven by police car (with a flashing red light) to the psychiatric hospital: the moment where she is abandoned by society to become the helpless victim of the monster. For Diane Long Hoeveler, the scene (and the film) 'ostensibly presents a black man's attempt to seize the power of the gaze, to seize the meaning of the narrative for himself, to make the film about him, his erotic pain and history' (2007: 100). The flash frames thus show both the Candyman's past and Helen's future, tied together in the Candyman's demand, 'Be my victim'. Hoeveler notes that what grips the viewer in this scene is Helen's eyes, 'the ambivalent combination in them of willingness and fear, desire and loathing' (ibid.). Helen will later seize back the gaze from the Candyman, effectively castrating him (as she does Trevor at the film's conclusion).

To achieve Helen's glassy-eyed responses during her encounters with the Candyman, Rose famously placed Virginia Madsen under hypnosis. Rose got the idea for this from Werner Herzog's *Heart of Glass* (1976) in which several of the cast were hypnotised before they went in front of the camera in order to affect a trance-like state. Rose wanted to control Madsen's performance during these scenes so as to avoid the stereotypical responses usually found in horror films when a woman reacts to the monster: 'When she saw him she would be hypnotised, as if in a trance, as if no longer in the real world' (Schwarz, 2004b). In terms of attempting to seize control of the woman's gaze, there are fascinating parallels with the on-screen narrative. It is not uncommon for directors to become involved in a Svengali-like relationship with their players during the filmmaking process. Madsen, at first, went along with the hypnosis in order to help her performance, but as got deeper into the filming, disliked the loss of agency and resisted (much as Helen later resists the Candyman's attempts to subjugate her). It can be argued that Madsen's own reclamation of the power of the gaze came to mirror Helen's in the film narrative.

There is indeed a mirroring/symmetry within the narrative itself at this point in the film as the story literally starts over. We are given a repeat of the film's opening shot of bees; and the Candyman's adjuring Helen ('come with me') signifies that only now is Helen's true journey about to begin, and that the repressed is inexorably returning.

'BE MY VICTIM'

As Kim Newman remarked in his 1993 review, *Candyman* 'combines an overall predictability' as Helen is drawn into the Candyman's dark place, with 'a-scene-to-scene sense of surprise as the plot progresses in daring leaps and ellipses which powerfully convey Helen's increasing bewilderment and fear'. The second half of *Candyman* – in contrast to its initial section, which revolves around hearsay (Helen gets closer to the source of the Candyman stories until they are totally disproven) – utilises conventional tropes of the horror-thriller in a similarly self-reflexive way to the film's use of urban myth. As Ebert identified, there is Helen as the 'Innocent Victim Wrongly Accused' of Hitchcock's films; and there are elements of the 1940s Paranoid Woman's picture in which the victim's claims of persecution are scornfully dismissed as fantasy or delusion. This, of course, evokes not only the Gothic paranoia of *Rebecca*, *Gaslight* (both 1940) and *Suspicion* (1941) but numerous other 1940s Hollywood films with plot elements of female madness, hysteria and amnesia. Mark Jancovich usefully defines the 1940s Paranoid Woman's picture:

> [T]hese films are claimed to be focused on a female lead but they are seen as paranoid due to the pervading sense of threat that these women experience, usually from a husband or lover. This focus on the feelings of terror experienced by the female protagonists, and on their persecution by men, often leads to these films being read as psychological narratives in which the perceptions of the central female are put under investigation. Narratively the woman herself is often uncertain whether to trust her own perceptions or not, and therefore often fears that she is going mad. (2007)

Candyman subverts the 1940s Paranoid Woman's film in several ways. Feminist critics such as Mary Ann Doane, according to Jancovich, have taken issue with films in the 1940s subgenre as they 'not only place their female protagonists in the role of victim, but turn the problem back onto these female characters, so that it is *their* psychology that is pathological' (ibid.). Although Rose plays with this trope in *Candyman*, we, the viewer, are never really in doubt that Helen is sane and that the Candyman is 'real'. In the Gothic paranoid films, as Doane herself comments, 'the cinematic apparatus itself seems mobilized against the female spectator, disabling her gaze' (1987a: 37). However, as Hoeveler notes with regard to *Candyman*, Helen, 'as academic researcher and postfeminist female Gothic detective… gazes back in such a dominating manner that instead she appears to take (back) control of the gaze' (2007: 100).

In the 1940s films, the woman is driven to the brink of madness 'less by the diabolical behaviour of others than by her own psychological inferiority' (Jancovich, 2007) and is 'revealed as impotent in terms of the actual ability to uncover the secret or attain the knowledge which she desires' (Doane, 1987b: 135). *Candyman* subverts this too, as Helen galvanises herself in the final act of the film, rejects the psychiatrist's opinion that she is delusional ('No matter what's going wrong… I know one thing – that no part of me... no matter how hidden, is capable of that') and determines to resolve her own problems. In the process she proves herself independent of male authority: her husband, the police, the psychiatrist and the Candyman.

Rose foregrounds narrative predictability and plot contrivance in a number of scenes. When Anne-Marie attacks Helen, whom she thinks is about to harm her child, Helen retaliates with a meat-cleaver, and the police burst in at the precise moment that Helen appears to incriminate herself. In this scene, and others that follow, Helen seems to fall victim to the narrative itself which in its leaps and ellipses slips completely from her control, creating surprise for the viewer and, as Newman observes, bewilderment for Helen. The narrative events of much of the second half serve to isolate and marginalise Helen in an attempt to disable her completely. The harrowing strip search that follows Helen's arrest might therefore be read less in terms of a ritual of defilement (although it contains all the hallmarks of one) than as a pointed commentary on the process by which male authority in *Candyman* seeks to disempower Helen as a woman (the screenplay states that Helen is 'humiliated and afraid').

Drawing on Kristeva, Barbara Creed has, as we know, written of the modern horror film as a form of modern defilement rite, working to 'separate out the Symbolic Order from all that threatens its stability, particularly the mother and all that her universe signifies... this means separating out the maternal authority from paternal law' (1986: 75). The body of the female in horror becomes the site of ritualistic defilement: she is slashed and mutilated, and polluted by decay, infection, disease, filth, pus, vomit, blood, etc. in order to 'eject the abject' maternal figure from the symbolic order, so that (in the words of Kuhn) the 'demarcation line between subject and that which threatens its existence can be redrawn more rigidly' (2000). In *Candyman*, Helen may be ritualistically defiled (drenched in blood, stripped, burned alive) but it can be interpreted (as I discuss later) that she is not finally relegated to her 'proper' (i.e. subjugated) place within the symbolic order, and instead establishes herself as the subject of the film's discourse and of the Candyman myth.

'I JUST BLACKED OUT AND WHEN I WOKE UP THERE WAS BLOOD EVERYWHERE'

The second half of *Candyman* follows a bookending, mirroring, repetitive structure in relation to the first half. Frank, the black detective, makes a re-appearance; his coldness towards Helen is in complete contrast to his friendly, supportive manner earlier. The absence of sympathy towards Helen by the cops in the second half (one of them calls her 'sick') shows how she is to become vilified, as was the Candyman. As a woman she is what society represses/oppresses, and this is to become manifest both to Helen and to us. Helen tries to phone Trevor at home, but he is not there. He has already abandoned her, in a sense. The camera focuses on Helen and Trevor's wedding photo, suggesting that the marriage will soon be over (it is intimated that Trevor is with his student lover, Stacey, when Helen tries to call him).

Rose's strategy of taking us into Helen's mind comes into its own here. We are shown baby Anthony in the Candyman's lair – the strobe lighting suggests that this is Helen's hallucination or 'vision', and the brief scene sets out Helen's motivation for later in the film: to defeat the Candyman and save the child. Before that, though, we must experience for ourselves Helen's increasing marginalisation by male authority; the process by which she is turned into the Other. After she is led through the gauntlet of reporters as the innocent person wrongly accused, Helen begins to suspect that Trevor disbelieves her story, despite his promise to stand by her. As she recounts her story to Trevor and her lawyer ('I just blacked out and when I woke up there was blood everywhere') she realises that Trevor may not be capable of the leap of faith necessary to overcome his doubts. Rose then cuts to Helen in the bath. It is another scene that invites intimacy and sympathetic identification between Helen and the viewer: Rose's idea of us 'being' with Helen, sharing in her nakedness and vulnerability. She attempts to cleanse herself after her ordeal. We are close on Helen's face – her hair is slicked back and she wears no make-up; she covers her breasts with her hands. There is a sense of her wanting to disguise her gender, the basis of her persecution.

We stay with her 'in the present tense' (as Rose describes it) as Helen tries to solve the mystery of the photograph in the next scene. She wants proof that the Candyman exists, so that she can convince Trevor and the authorities that her story is true. Like the protagonists in Dario Argento's giallo thrillers, Helen, the investigator, is trying to solve a mystery whose answer is located *within* the self. As Rose has commented 'what she wants to confront is really something that's inside her'. She wants to prove (to herself and others) that she didn't commit murder and that the Candyman must therefore exist.

It is intriguing, then, that the Candyman appears so shockingly so soon afterwards. It is another 'daring leap' in the narrative, but one that seems to have been willed by Helen herself. Kuhn describes the Candyman as Helen's tool: 'his presence helps her create a story that places herself at the very heart of the narrative'. By consciously invoking the Candyman she begins to 'bridge her real-life powerlessness'; thus the more she is put under pressure by the events of the narrative, 'the more we see of the "hook-man"' (2000). His intrusion into Helen's 'real' world is marked here by use of the hand-held camera to indicate this instability, this queasy merging of realities. The Candyman exhibits a supernatural ability to appear in different places, transcending physical possibility. There is the sense of the noose tightening as the Candyman cuts off Helen's every avenue of escape, so the story increasingly becomes the 'insane Kafkaesque nightmare' intended by Rose in his screenplay (1991: 54).

The film, at the same time, explores the ways in which Helen and the Candyman are 'visually, physically and ideologically linked, rather than opposed' (Donaldson, 2011: 40). In other words, the film's discourse(s) on race, gender and class become intertwined and embodied by both Helen and the Candyman. As Lucy Donaldson states, 'both are framed as slave and victim, both exploited by the capitalist structures of white patriarchy and involved in transgressing such boundaries' (2011: 39). This focus on the relationship between Helen and the Candyman increasingly marginalises other characters, such as Bernadette, who, by contrast, ultimately becomes little more than the archetypal horror film 'best friend' whose role is, in Rose's words, 'to die'. And Bernadette's death by the hook brings with it a further association of rape, making this element of *Candyman* symptomatic of the 'reactionary inflection' that Wood talks of as being inherent in the genre.

'A strange affinity between monster and woman':The Candyman (Tony Todd) and Helen (Virginia Madsen)

'NO PART OF ME, NO MATTER HOW HIDDEN, IS CAPABLE OF THAT'

Through the adoption/subversion of the Paranoid Woman narrative we are in sympathy with Helen, and yet the other characters cannot be. We know that she is not insane because we understand her, and therefore we know she is persecuted. After Bernadette's murder, we cut to the flashing blue light and Helen in the police car being taken to an institution. The film places us, alongside Helen, in a state of abjection – we are to be locked away from society with Helen. This is the moment the film has been building up to. A flash frame of the Candyman mural again links Helen with the Candyman as the persecuted/ostracised deemed by society to be Other. Rose again cuts to baby Anthony in the womb-like lair of the Candyman. As Kuhn notes, 'the "feminine" interiors of Cabrini-Green appear as the actual inner world or subconscious fantasy' of Helen (2000): here linking to the idea of birth-death-rebirth as we cut back to Helen's point of view as the police car comes out of a tunnel (birth canal?) into the light.

Rose continues the subjective camera work in the hospital scene as Helen is sectioned. We see Helen's point of view of the ceiling – strip lights strobe past – and Trevor's concerned face as he accompanies Helen who is strapped to a gurney. Rose emphasises the physical separation of the couple as the orderlies wheel Helen away. Her social isolation is further underlined by her being bound and strapped to a bed in the psychiatric hospital's solitary confinement wing. The theme of insanity (key to psychological horror) is here a metaphor for being cast off as Other by a society unsympathetic to difference. 'They will all abandon you', the Candyman warns Helen, as he materialises again, floating above her. Helen is now effectively alone with the Candyman, unable to move or defend herself, which is where she 'belongs' (or so he tries to convince her). 'You have seen the invisible and experienced the irrational – they have not' (Rose, 1991: 71).

Jancovich notes how the Paranoid Woman's film subjects its female protagonist 'not simply to a controlling male gaze, but to a medical gaze' (2007). This is literalised in *Candyman* when Helen is shown a CCTV recording of herself reacting to the Candyman, who is not there. The purpose of the medical gaze in the Paranoid Woman's film has been interpreted as an attempt to dominate and control female subjectivity. In this case, the psychiatrist Dr. Burke tries to convince Helen that she is delusional, that the Candyman exists only in her mind, and that she is therefore 'psychologically incapable of making sense of the world around her, and unable to trust her own perceptions' (ibid.). Madsen's performance distils the scripted scene perfectly, as she is momentarily flooded with self-doubt ('I killed my best friend… she trusted me… she loved me… I cut her open… I… It's not possible… it's…') before demonstrating an inner strength, an unshakable self-knowledge ('No part of me, no matter how hidden, is capable of that'). Hence when she then invokes the Candyman, who proceeds to gut the psychiatrist, it is a vindication of sorts, one that allows Helen to escape. The Candyman cuts her shackles: it is he, rather than the psychiatrist, who becomes her ally at this point in the film. (It is striking how Helen's daring escape from the psychiatric institution resembles that of Sarah Connor in *Terminator 2: Judgement Day* [1991]. Helen, along with Sarah Connor and Ripley in *Aliens* (1986), might be seen a prototype horror-SF action heroine.)

'THEY WILL ALL ABANDON YOU'

Helen returns home, where she confronts Trevor, who has already moved his student mistress into the apartment. 'What's the matter, Trevor? Scared of something?,' she asks, realising that her husband is afraid of her and what she might do to him. Although bereft, Helen also glimpses true power for the first time; the kind of power that the Candyman has. Anger follows, and then the realisation that she is well and truly alone: 'You were all I had left,' she tells Trevor. Grief and then acceptance: 'It's over.' Madsen's performance again is such that we are taken through these emotions vividly and believably, moving us along Helen's journey towards transcendence.

The screenplay next shows Helen contemplating suicide in the Chicago river. 'She stands regarding the dirty water swirling below her,' Rose writes. 'A jump and it would all be over. Someone else's problem.' The screenplay makes it clear that Helen 'has made the decision to die' (1991: 81). But then she remembers the Candyman telling her that he is going to kill the baby, Anthony. This memory stops Helen from attempting suicide, and fills her with a newfound sense of purpose as she determines to save the child from the Candyman. As written it is an unconvincing scene, too great a 'U-turn' to work dramatically. In the film, however, the meaning of the scene is subtly different: it no longer presents suicide as an option; rather the scene is about Helen's coming to terms with the realisation that she is out in the cold, isolated and alone. The scene as filmed makes Helen stronger because it shows her processing her new-found understanding of herself and her place in society (or more accurately, her status as an outsider), rather than deciding whether or not to die. We then see that she has galvanised herself to act autonomously in her decision to save the child. In other words, she is stronger in the film than in the screenplay where she had contemplated suicide. At the same time, by still affording Helen a decision-making space in the narrative (where in essence, she determines once and for all not to be the victim), the film emphasises Helen's autonomy more forcefully. Again, we can see this as a subversion of the Paranoid Woman's film whereby the heroine is 'unable to resolve her own problems' (Jancovich, 2007).

'A jump and it would all be over': Helen (Virginia Madsen) contemplates her fate in Candyman

'COME WITH ME, AND BE IMMORTAL'

In the film's third Act, Helen must move through liminal space and time to enter the Candyman's world, as he has entered hers. Rose intercuts the actual Cabrini-Green with Helen entering the Candyman's forbidden chamber, juxtaposing prosaic reality with liminal action: Helen is moving into a parallel world in her bid for individuation; her journey progressing from (self) knowledge to power to transcendence. Rose presents us with more rebirth imagery during Helen's journey; the bloody chamber as the uterus. Helen seizes the hook (phallus) hanging in the chamber. Paintings in the Candyman's lair show the Candyman's story: his lynching and his progress towards a form of sainthood (this prefigures Helen's own journey towards becoming legend). Helen attempts to seize the power from Candyman – his hook – but she is hypnotised again – and he instead seizes *her*.

There then takes place a seduction scene that Barker himself has described as 'repulsive': as the Candyman embraces Helen, he opens his chest and the bees come out. It is an explicit reference to the Lyle's Golden Syrup motif of the partially rotten lion: 'out of the strong came forth sweetness'. Rose's implication here may be that the Candyman's strength shall be passed on to Helen in her transcendent state, and her vindication shall be the 'sweetness'. Some critics have, however, suggested that the body horror operating in the sequence serves to undermine the acceptability of *Candyman*'s central relationship. Isabel Pinedo observes that 'as the interracial romance of the past once conjured up disgust and loathing in the white mob, so the suggestion of intimate contact with Candyman conjures up body horror in the white mob' (1997: 131). Indeed, the ways in which the bees crawl over the prone Helen also evokes the defilement ritual. There is then an interesting dissolve to the baby, and with it the suggestion of miscegenation.

'IT WAS ALWAYS YOU, HELEN'

Helen awakens. The Candyman has taken baby Anthony. On the wall, the Candyman has also left Helen a message: 'It was always you, Helen.' There is an essential ambiguity to this statement. As discussed earlier, Helen is, in the words of Kim Hester-Williams, 'ensnared by both an indirect and direct identification with the white landowner's daughter of the legend' whom she physically resembles. Indeed, in the screenplay Rose writes of the young woman in the mural (which depicts the Candyman's death) that 'we see the young woman's face: it is Helen'. In other words, it is suggested that Helen is the actual reincarnation of the white landowner's daughter with whom the Candyman fell in love. This, of course, provides the Candyman with his motivation throughout the film: Helen reminds him of his lost love (or is, in fact, his lost love reborn). However, 'It was always you, Helen' also conveys the idea that Helen's destiny was always to be the transcendent being she becomes at the film's conclusion. The resemblance between Helen and the landowner's daughter thus links Helen to the horror of nineteenth-century slavery in ways that Hester-Williams contends, so that Helen's transformation 'into the Candyman' (as Hester-Williams puts it) is to carry on 'the haunting of all those who would refuse to (re)member him – that is, to (re)member the slave past' (2004: 4). This is reinforced in the screenplay where Rose states that the mural scene of Candyman's lynching is reproduced to the exact detail when Helen crawls from the bonfire aflame later in the film and 'men hold her down'.

Although associated with Guy Fawkes in Barker's 'The Forbidden', the bonfire in *Candyman* thereby takes on associations of lynchings and burnings at the stake of Blacks in the South in the nineteenth and early twentieth centuries. The residents set it alight because Jake mistakes Helen (who still carries the hook) for the Candyman. The residents want to destroy the Candyman; they rise up en masse against his tyranny. Rose frames their mobilisation as a visual formation emphasising their solidarity. We see the angry faces of the residents; they are individualised in the sequence. Peter Hutchings is therefore not entirely correct in his assertion that no collectivity is shown amongst the Cabrini-Green residents in the film prior to Helen's funeral. This sequence shows them as a collective attempting to vanquish their oppressor, the Candyman (which is, of course, an ambiguous message in itself).

Inside the raging bonfire, the Candyman tries to claim Helen as his own, pinning her arms in an attempt to immobilise her so that she might die and join him in his world. Helen demonstrates her defiance by staking the Candyman like a vampire (how many women in horror films ever get to stake a vampire?) so that he can be destroyed. Helen's final defilement is to be made physically monstrous and deformed by her scarring in the fire; her burning in this way again links Helen to the lynching of the Candyman as a symbol of Black oppression.

The Candyman (Tony Todd) traps Helen (Virginia Madsen) inside the blazing bonfire

'WHAT'S THE MATTER, TREVOR? SCARED OF SOMETHING?'

Kuhn suggests that Helen's becoming an abject herself can be interpreted in two ways. We might read the film's ending as 'the punishment of the active female subject' who is transformed into a passive object 'so that the order she disrupted can be re-established'. This reading would posit Helen's becoming, in her resurrected avenging angel persona at the end of the film, an example of Creed's Monstrous-Feminine. Helen, having usurped the traditional male positions of narrative agent and investigator 'is punished and relegated to her "proper" place within the symbolic'. However, Helen's defeat of the Candyman (and her punishment of Trevor) might also suggest that she is not finally subjugated to the symbolic order. As Kuhn notes, the film offers a second possible reading, in which:

> Helen is not denigrated to the object of the monster's desire, but instead establishes herself as the subject of the film's discourse and of the Candyman myth. In that case the Candyman cannot be interpreted as a representation of male fetishism… but as the manifestation of a woman's desire for power and subjectivity. (2000)

This second reading is supported by the actions of the Cabrini-Green residents at Helen's funeral. The dispossessed symbolically pass on the hook (an icon of phallic power) to Helen.

Anne-Marie McCoy (Vanessa Williams) leads a procession of Cabrini-Green residents to Helen's funeral

Trevor (Xander Berkeley), wracked with guilt

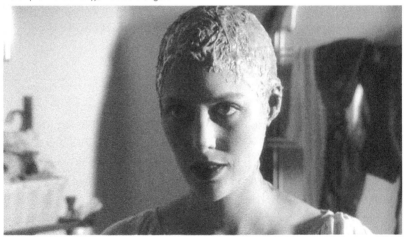

Helen (Virginia Madsen) 'becomes myth' in Candyman

The film's final scene, in which Trevor unwittingly summons Helen's spirit who exacts bloody retribution, is not present in the revised screenplay dated August 1991. In an email to the author (23 April, 2017) Rose confirmed that:

There was originally a shorter version of the ending as it stands. We then decided to go for a more poetic ending with Helen walled up behind her mural, but eventually went back and reshot the ending as per the original idea (somewhat expanded) as the film needed to put the idea of Helen becoming myth herself with more energy.

All the versions say the same thing though – that she becomes the myth.

Helen's becoming the Candyman myth can be read as her embodying 'a woman's desire for power and subjectivity', as Kuhn claims. More widely, though, it is a reaffirmation of urban myth itself; a recapitulation of the film's central motif. Trevor's guilt and desire for punishment triggers Helen's return; just as white liberal guilt triggered the return of the Candyman. In the words of Kirsten Moana Thompson, '*Candyman* suggests that oral storytelling and, by extension, urban legends are valuable forms of historical memory, and that the process of historical amnesia will be apocalyptic' (2007: 59). The Candyman is a return of the repressed, as is Helen. The final image of the film depicts a new mural in the Candyman's lair, that of Helen herself 'rising from the bonfire like a phoenix, her hair aflame like a halo' (Rose, 1991: 94). She has achieved a state of transcendence.

CONCLUSIONS

The film's appropriation of Robin Wood's Return of the Repressed thesis does not necessarily constitute a progressive text in and of itself, of course. As Sharrett has stated, neoconservative horror of the 1990s sought to co-opt horror's radicalism as part of capitalism's re-legitimation; it is possible to argue therefore that the Return of the Repressed schema can operate within the framework of neoconservative horror. In the case of *Candyman*, a number of critics have reasoned along these lines, and I conclude this chapter with a consideration given to some of their contentions.

Laura Wyrick makes the point that horror comes not simply from the return of the repressed as much as from the 'circularity of the process of repression, return and recuperation… history demands the acknowledgement and recuperation of its own excessive discourses' (1998: 113). A number of critics dispute *Candyman* as a progressive horror film for this reason; Pinedo, for example, concludes that 'in the end, *Candyman* depicts both the white woman and the black man as monstrous' (1997: 131). Hoeveler contends that *Candyman* reveals how difficult it is 'to tell anything but thoroughly sexist, racist and classist narratives, even when the authors are well intentioned liberals who ostensibly want to expose those very crimes in their works'. For Hoeveler, it is the 'sheer negative weight of ideologies about the connection between white women and black men' that creates this difficulty (2007: 100). Hester-Williams offers a similar conclusion when she writes that films such as *Candyman* suggest that 'American popular culture continues to perpetuate the cultural myth that we are, all of us, slaves' (2004: 43). Indeed, the film's central association of 'oppressed' white middle-class females with historical Black experience has been much criticised, particularly by recent writers.

In his 2016 book *Magical Thinking, Fantastic Film, and the Illusions of Neoliberalism*, Michael J. Blouin explicitly links *Candyman* with neoliberal racism, arguing that it is a specific tendency of apparently subversive narratives to reaffirm a problematic treatment of race. According to Blouin, horror films of this type attempt to expose the viewer to his or her prejudices 'through a seemingly significant reversal: the monster is not outside, but within; the terror is not blackness, but whiteness'. The message of these films is that 'racism can be overcome'. Blouin, however, goes on to note that such commercial works transform race into another commodity 'upon which entrepreneurial subjects might capitalise' thereby perpetuating the tenets of racialist thinking they initially purport to critique. Although on the surface, *Candyman* reverses and undermines racist perspectives – Helen transforms into the monster at the end – 'in truth', writes Blouin, 'this faux reversal extends an underlying imbalance of power. It also shifts attention from the real (and persistent) legacy of racism to the playfulness of racialism.' Blouin argues that by offering the 'gift of antiracialism' to audiences in this way, 'even more potent forms of racism' are smuggled into the culture.

The crux of Blouin's argument is that because *Candyman* moves to 'diminish divisions between a black man and a white woman' by casting their difference as superficial, it 'wilfully overlooks crucial distinctions between the material circumstances of these groups'. Thus, for Blouin, a text such as *Candyman* offers merely 'illusory progress': the result being that 'alternatives – including a better understanding of the idea of race, divorced from its imbrication within the conditions of Homo economicus – gradually fade from public discourse'. *Candyman*, Blouin concludes, 'rotates the axis of color without actually challenging its modus operandi' (Blouin, 2016: 81-91).

Although central to the narrative of *Candyman*, making a white woman the focus of a film that ostensibly tackles the subject of racism remains, for many critics, problematic. Others who have given close attention to the film's gender-based approach appreciate the film for its fresh perspective on the old story of monster and victim, for the way Helen is able to rewrite the story and make herself the hero. They might argue at least that *Candyman* is a female-centric horror film, even if the nature and extent of its feminism is up for debate.

Indeed, the value of *Candyman* may ultimately lie in its complex and contradictory treatment of difference, as Balasopoulos contends; the ways in which it questions the boundaries of race, gender and class identity in modern America. These ambiguities, of course, leave the film open to further interpretations.

5. Sequels, Spin-offs and Knock-offs

> It's really a shame that ['Bride of Candyman'] story was never continued. If someone ever let me do a sequel that's the direction I would take it. (Bernard Rose, email to author, 23 April, 2017)

In October 2016 social media was rife with the rumour that Bernard Rose was at work on a new sequel to *Candyman*, one which would see the return of Virginia Madsen as Helen and take place either immediately after the original or feature the same characters twenty years later. As Rose told Lola Landekic at *Art of the Title*:

> I would love to make a proper sequel. There are all sorts of reasons why it's never happened… I don't control the rights, otherwise I would just do it.

The legalities of the *Candyman* franchise have grown ever more complex over the years as the chain of title has passed from company to company. According to Tony Todd, ownership of the franchise went first from Propaganda Films to Sony, then to Columbia, and finally to Artisan and Lion's Gate. (A fourth sequel – without Rose's involvement – was briefly mooted in 2004 but never came about due to these licensing issues.) At a Q&A that took place at York's City Screen Picturehouse in November 2016, Rose confirmed that he had been in talks with Clive Barker (who would return as executive producer) over a mooted sequel but that the rights were 'complicated'.

There is indeed suggestion that the time would be right for a new *Candyman* film – one helmed by Rose – given the surge of female-centric horror in recent years (*The Babadook* [2014] *The Love Witch* and *Raw* [both 2016]) and the phenomenal box office of *Get Out* (2017), a film that allegorises (and satirises) white liberal America's co-optation of black identity.

Rose, in fact, wrote a sequel to *Candyman* back in the 1990s. Propaganda Films was contractually obliged to have him author the draft – but then rejected it. Rose (who has had no subsequent involvement with the franchise) described his original sequel as similar in concept to Alan Moore's graphic novel, *From Hell* (which was adapted into a film of the same name by the Hughes brothers in 2001): the story went back in time and was set in London circa Jack the Ripper. Rose has said that the idea was discarded simply because it was 'not right'. Barker, however, claims that Rose had been 'driven crazy' by the studio's script demands ('Well, what we need is a scene like this, a scene like that') in its desire to replicate *Candyman*'s success, concluding that what the studio had really wanted all along was '*Candyman* 1 with the names changed' (Schwartz, 2004b).

In many ways, the two extant sequels – *Candyman: Farewell to the Flesh* and *Candyman: Day of the Dead* – fall into this trap: each attempts to deliver more of the same but arguably without the level of intelligence and skill that Rose brought to the original. Neither is without interest, however, and this final chapter begins with a consideration of both before going on to survey a number of films influenced by *Candyman* and urban myths (in particular the 'Bloody Mary' legend).

CANDYMAN: FAREWELL TO THE FLESH (BILL CONDON, 1995)

In the DVD commentary of *Candyman* Barker described the sequel as 'a painful process', largely because of the conservatism of the studio in wanting to rehash the original. Barker's stated intention with *Candyman: Farewell to the Flesh* was 'to enrich the mythology of the first film… this movie will answer a lot of questions that were left unanswered at the end of the first *Candyman* picture' (French, 1995). The sequel clarifies the origins of the Candyman (here given the name Daniel Robitaille), but also the miscegenation subtext of the first film is made more explicit.

Director Bill Condon (who has since gone on to become a major player with the *Twilight* saga and *Beauty and the Beast*) brings a workman-like approach to the material, although the film largely avoids the televisual blandness of the second sequel, *Candyman: Day of the Dead*. Having said that, both suffer from an over-reliance on the jump scare (a technique that undoubtedly contributed to the box office success of the first film, and which the filmmakers try to repeat here). The effect, though, is to make the sequels formulaic.

A derivative approach is apparent from the opening sequence of *Farewell to the Flesh* in which Michael Culkin makes his reappearance as Purcell only to be despatched by the Candyman before the titles commence: a convention familiar from 1980s slashers such as *Friday 13th Part 2* (1981). But this opening also sets up the premise. Purcell informs us that the Candyman myth is a mobile one: the Candyman relocates to troubled places. One such place is shown to be New Orleans, where *Farewell to the Flesh* is set. Condon devotes considerable time to semi-documentary footage of the poor black areas of the city. A theme of the film is the flooding that threatens New Orleans, in particular those living in the centre, i.e. the poorer residents (the middle-classes – including middle-class blacks – moved out of the city centre to newer housing in the 1950s and 1960s). This is clearly intended as a reference to the failure of drainage and flood control during Hurricane Betsy in 1965 which resulted in the deaths of dozens of people. (It is impossible to watch the film now without also thinking of the disastrous flooding from Hurricane Katrina in 2005, which particularly affected the city's poor black residents, both during and after the event.) The climax of the film fittingly takes place as the Mississippi bursts its banks, threatening again to wash away the dispossessed.

Candyman: Farewell to the Flesh reprises the motif of a white female protagonist who functions as detective, this time in the form of schoolteacher Annie Tarrant (Kelly Rowan), daughter of a wealthy New Orleans businessman murdered by the Candyman for reasons Annie attempts to uncover. Annie's commitment to educating the poor black children of New Orleans signals the film's white liberal agenda from the outset. Annie discovers during the course of the story that she is the descendent of the Candyman; the film clarifies that the white landowner's daughter whom Daniel made pregnant (named Caroline Sullivan in the sequel) herself had a daughter (the film names her Isabel), and that Daniel's lineage therefore continues within the 'white' family that had effectively murdered him. Diane Long Hoeveler observes that *Farewell to the Flesh* attempts to present an 'allegory of the hidden life of miscegenation in American society' (2007: 110), and, in this respect, the New Orleans setting of the film lends it further significance.

In the years before the American Civil War, Louisiana housed more free people of colour than perhaps any other state, with New Orleans, in particular, home to artisans and middle-class blacks with property living alongside (and in some cases owning) African slaves. The free people of colour were mainly mixed race. 'Miscegenation in the South,' as Hoeveler comments, 'has long been an established fact of life' (2007: 111). Towards the end of the Reconstruction, however, the Democrats introduced the Jim Crow laws which disenfranchised blacks, including freed slaves and monied mixed-race people, and brought in racial segregation in the South which continued until the mid-1960s.

Significantly, the lynching of Daniel Robitaille (Todd), as Rose tells us in the first film, took place in 1890, the year that the Jim Crow laws were introduced. *Candyman: Farewell to the Flesh* returns to this lynching graphically throughout the film; the passing of the Jim Crow laws starting in 1890 thus becomes the film's 'allegorical moment' – dramatised in the murder of Robitaille for his act of miscegenation. Hoeveler describes *Farewell to the Flesh* as coming down 'firmly on the side of liberal acceptance of miscegenation and the intermixing of the races' (2007: 110) However, its message in terms of the acknowledgement of history by a white audience is ambiguous.

Daniel Robitaille (Tony Todd) is smothered in honey and stung to death by bees in Candyman: Farewell to the Flesh *(1995)*

This ambiguity becomes apparent in the film's concluding scene. After destroying the Candyman in a confrontation that takes place in the abandoned Sullivan plantation (designated by Hoeveler as 'the white enclave of power that had excluded and then exterminated Daniel' [2007: 110]), the action cuts to several years later: Annie now has a (markedly Caucasian) daughter called Caroline. Annie shows her photographs of her ancestors, including of Daniel Robitaille, whom she freely acknowledges as her daughter's 'great-great-grandfather'. However, when Caroline later tries to invoke the

Candyman, Annie stops her. It seems that miscegenation can be recuperated into the white liberal identity but the 'curse' of racism (the hatred that created the Candyman) and culpability for it cannot. Annie's simultaneous acknowledgement of Daniel as her ancestor and her repudiation of the Candyman equates to a denial of history itself – a refutation of the racial segregation, black disenfranchisement and racist violence that took place in America between 1890 and 1960. (This ambiguity is even apparent in the film's title: 'farewell to the flesh' suggests that Annie – and, by extension, the viewer – is willing to accept her blood relationship with the 'good' Daniel, but not the 'evil' Candyman.)

But little Caroline's attempt to invoke the Candyman also suggests that as history this truth cannot be repressed or excluded. It – and the Candyman – will inexorably return.

CANDYMAN: DAY OF THE DEAD (TURI MEYER, 1999)

Candyman: Farewell to the Flesh was a financial and critical failure, a case of 'diminishing artistic returns', as *Variety* (March 16, 1995) described it. Critics noted how the social commentary of the original had become lost in a welter of graphic violence and jump scares, 'drowning a potent metaphor for African American rage and oppression' (*Los Angeles Times*, March 20, 1995). However, the film was a success on cable and in the VHS rental market; this spurred a second sequel in 1999.

Released straight to DVD by Artisan Entertainment, *Candyman: Day of the Dead* is essentially a remake of the original film, with certain plot elements of *Farewell to the Flesh* thrown in to the mix. Instead of Chicago/New Orleans, the setting is now Downtown Los Angeles; Mardi Gras becomes Día de Muertos, the Latin festival of remembrance for loved ones who have died. The implicit denial of racism that characterised the first sequel is even more apparent in *Day of the Dead*; here the 'problem' of racism is confined to individuals, in this case, two bad cops in the Los Angeles Police Department; there is little sense in the film's wider depiction of everyday life in Los Angeles of the lingering racial (and class) tensions that led to the Watts riots, the Rodney King beatings, and the 1992 riots. But if race and class are no longer issues in America, as the film seems to suggest, if these problems have been eradicated, then the Candyman himself becomes obsolete: indeed the central concern of the plot of *Day of the Dead* is an attempt to erase the Candyman myth from the cultural consciousness once and for all.

The protagonist with this in mind is Caroline McKeever (Donna D'Errico), who, as a small child in *Farewell to the Flesh* was forbidden from invoking the Candyman myth by her mother, Annie Tarrant. Caroline remains traumatised by her mother's subsequent suicide (Annie was in fact murdered by the Candyman whom she continued to deny) and seeks closure through her attempts to dispel the urban myth surrounding her great-great grandfather, Daniel Robitaille (Todd); to have him accepted instead as a great painter. This she initially tries to do by exhibiting Daniel's work in a trendy Downtown art gallery, organised by gallery owner, Miguel (Mark Adai-Rios), and his Hispanic actor friend, David (Jsu Garcia) with whom Caroline forms a close attachment. However, when Miguel is murdered by the Candyman, and David subsequently abducted by him (in an attempt to persuade Caroline to give up her life so that she and the Candyman can be together) suspicion again falls on the Candyman's 'victim', in this case Caroline.

In the DVD booklet of *Candyman: Day of the Dead*, director and co-writer Meyer (who would go on to a career in television) claims that in the film 'we get a much deeper understanding of the pathos of what the Candyman went through… we see what was taken away from him and we understand what he wants to reclaim – his family'. However, in truth, *Day of the Dead* adds little to deepen our understanding of the character. Instead, Meyer repeats the now-familiar *Candyman* tropes by-the-numbers. The most original aspects of the film are its occasional pop-surreal touches, such as the opening nightmare sequence, which takes place in a pristine white bathroom; in a later scene a bee emerges in giant close-up from a newly-cracked egg; and the Candyman's entrance, which happens in an empty subway, has the hook-man float in through a train-tunnel flanked by a swarm of bees. In this respect, *Candyman: Day of the Dead* owes more perhaps to the *Nightmare on Elm Street* franchise and nineties supernatural TV drama such as *Buffy: The Vampire Slayer* (1997-2003), *Angel* (1999-2004) and *Charmed* (1998-2006), than it does to the original *Candyman*. Indeed, the film utilises in many of its scenes the exact kind of 'crappy blue back light' that Rose claims to despise in 'bad '80s horror movies' (*Candyman* DVD commentary, 2005).

The Candyman (Tony Todd) appears in a subway in Candyman: Day of the Dead

Candyman: Day of the Dead concludes with Caroline destroying the Candyman whose murders are pinned, implausibly, on one of the racist cops (whom we are told had a history of mental illness). Thus, Caroline is able to debunk the Candyman myth finally: 'No-one will ever call your name again. There's no such thing as the Candyman.' The ending sees Caroline reunited with her lover David and his daughter Christine at a picnic by Annie's grave, in celebration of Día de Muertos. Caroline is finally at peace with the loss of her mother, and the Candyman has been vanquished, at least for the time being.

Whilst the 'problem' of race is ironed out in *Candyman: Day of the Dead* by simple virtue of being ignored (ignore it and it no longer exists), in following the general trajectory of the franchise, the issue of gender is similarly reversed. If the Helen of *Candyman* was, in the words of Andrea Kuhn, 'active bearer of the look' (2000), then Caroline in *Day of the Dead* is, by contrast, passive object of the male gaze. Meyer's camera reduces D'Errico (star of TV's *Baywatch* and a former *Playboy* magazine Playmate of the Month) to little more than a Barbie-doll (which, ironically, creates a degree of sympathy for D'Errico as she struggles with the thankless role). She is, to quote Diane Long Hoeveler, 'very white and very blonde' (2007: 110), and fetishised throughout the film, not least by the Candyman in his obsessive pursuit of her. In all, the complex and contradictory problematic of difference that *Candyman* presented is neutralised in the sequels. *Candyman: Farewell to the Flesh* and *Candyman: Day of the Dead* no longer question received notions about difference; indeed they seem to warn *against* questioning those notions. The Candyman shall not be invoked; and his 'evil' must be repudiated.

If, according to the filmmakers themselves, the Candyman should not exist, which is the message conveyed by the two sequels (to have him exist is to raise troublesome issues of race, class and gender), then this may cast further light on why no new instalment in the franchise has been produced. It also begs the question: if the franchise *were* to continue – with the Candyman as the central character – what direction could it possibly take? We might perhaps look to Tony Todd, as co-producer of the sequels, for an answer to this. In a commentary recorded for the *Candyman* DVD in 2005, Todd made some interesting remarks about where he would like the role to go:

> I would like to see a descendent of Candyman, played by me, a professor of a small college perhaps, who's been denying this linkage somehow. It gets revisited through the investigations of a new student; something to be explored about Candyman having to come back to battle an evil that may be perceived as greater than he is. I want to explore some heroic things and then (have) a cataclysmic battle.

The notion of the Candyman fighting an evil greater than he, of doing 'heroic things', is intriguing; as is the prospect of Todd playing the dual roles of professor and the Candyman, suggesting a possible recasting of Otherness. Robin Wood has spoken of the horror genre's 'essential dilemma' – which resides in the relationship between the monster and normality – and the implications thereof: 'Can the genre survive the recognition that the monster is its real hero? If the "return of the repressed" is conceived in positive terms, what happens to "horror"? And is such a positive conception logically possible?' (2003: 97). It would be interesting to see if Todd can indeed portray the Candyman in positive terms (as I write this, Todd's take on the Candyman – whatever it may be – has yet to transpire).

URBAN LEGEND FRANCHISE

Although the *Candyman* franchise stalled with *Day of the Dead* in 1999, other films in the 2000s have consciously incorporated urban myths in their storylines, most notably movies in the *Urban Legend* series.

Urban Legend (1998) concerns a killer (Rebecca Gayheart) on campus of a New England university whose murder methods directly imitate urban myths: a character is axed by an assailant hiding in the back seat of her car; another is forced to consume pop rocks and Coca-Cola until his stomach explodes; the protagonist, Natalie (played by Alicia Witt), has her stomach cut open by the killer who attempts to steal her kidney; and so on.

As a meta-slasher *Urban Legend* owes more to the slick teen horror of *Scream* (1996) and *I Know What You Did Last Summer* (1998) than it does to urban myth. The urban legends themselves provide little more than novelty killings in a generic plotline. Indeed, by placing popular urban myths in quotation marks, as the film does, much of their power is lost. Again, to cite *Halloween*, Carpenter's film is built upon variations of popular urban myth themes, constituting a re-telling of urban myth in cinematic form; it is itself folkloric in function. *Urban Legend*, on the other hand, directly quotes actual urban legends, replays them slavishly in its plot, but lacks the cultural context to give those urban legends resonance.

Urban Legend was poorly received by critics but enough of a box office success for Columbia/Sony to produce a sequel in 2000. *Urban Legends: Final Cut* places even more distance between itself and the urban legends it (ostensibly) draws upon. Taking as its central premise a film student making a film about a serial killer using urban legends, it is a movie about a movie about urban myth! This sense of remove only serves to highlight that *Final Cut* is, however, fundamentally little more than a series of bizarre death scenes in an unconvincing meta-narrative that borrows heavily from other popular movies (most notably the superior *Final Destination* franchise).

By contrast, the third film in the *Urban Legend* series, the 2005 straight-to-video release *Urban Legends: Bloody Mary*, moves away from the serial killer premise of previous *Urban Legend* entries in favour of a supernatural plotline. *Urban Legends: Bloody Mary* takes inspiration directly from the Mary legend, updating the myth and re-telling it within the framework of teen movie horror.

The film opens in Salt Lake City in 1969. At her High School Prom, Mary Banner (Lillith Fields) and her two friends Gina (Haley McCormick) and Grace (Tina Lifford) are slipped Rohypnol by their dates. As Grace and Gina are hustled into a car, Mary flees back into the school where she hides in a utility room. Her boyfriend (who is unnamed until the twist ending of the film) follows, and in a violent confrontation, Mary falls and strikes her head. Thinking she is dead, the boyfriend bundles Mary into a trunk where she eventually suffocates. After this expository prologue we move to present day as Mary's story is told by three friends (one of whom is the film's protagonist Samantha, played by Kate Mara) at a sleep-over. The tale as related by the girls essentially becomes a recasting of the Bloody Mary legend. 'Her rotting body's still there waiting to be discovered,' we are informed. 'If you go into the bathroom and turn off the lights and chant Bloody Mary three times into the mirror she appears. Her face is like a corpse. And if you look at her, you have to turn the lights back on before she drags you in… or she'll haunt you for ever.'

Samantha (Kate Mara, middle) and her friends Martha (Hailey Smith) and Mindy (Olesya Rulin) recount the legend of Bloody Mary in Urban Legends: Bloody Mary *(2005)*

The three friends chant 'Bloody Mary', and we see an apparition outside the house. Next morning, Samantha's step-dad Bill (Ed Marinaro) and mum Pam (Nancy Everhard) find the girls gone. The police are called; the girls are eventually found in an old abandoned mill, unhurt, but with traces of Rohypnol in their systems. They don't remember how they got there, but suspicion falls on school football player Buck (Michael Coe) and his friends. When these boys are murdered one-by-one, Samantha and her brother David (Robert Vito) set out to find the killer. Their investigations lead them to the mystery of the original girls' disappearance from the prom in 1969, and the truth behind Mary Banner's death.

Urban Legends: Bloody Mary's developmental sequences, like those of *Urban Legend* and *Final Cut*, owe much to the *Final Destination* movies. In a scene taken directly from *Final Destination 3* (2006), one of Buck's friends finds himself trapped inside a tanning bed, and is burned to a cinder. Another is fatally electrocuted when he urinates on an electrified fence ('Holy shit, this guy's dick is smoking,' exclaims a paramedic). In keeping with the franchise's basic premise, Bloody Mary herself is able to mobilise urban myths in her bid to exact revenge on her enemies: in the film's most effective (and disgusting) death, a spider burrows under the skin of an unsuspecting victim to lay its eggs; later the unfortunate girl's face literally erupts with tiny arachnids.

As the synopsis suggests, *Urban Legends: Bloody Mary* owes a greater debt to *Candyman* than do the previous *Urban Legend* entries: director Mary Lambert and her screenwriters acknowledge this intratextually when Samantha initially exclaims of the Bloody Mary legend, 'That's not even a real urban legend – that's just like that movie *Candyman*'. (Later, the filmmakers have a character offer the rebuke, '*Candyman* ripped off Bloody Mary in the first place, not the other way around!')

Mary's death appears in flash-back several times in the film, much like Robitaille's lynching is revisited obsessively in the *Candyman* movies. In *Urban Legends: Bloody Mary* date-rape takes the place of *Candyman*'s racist violence as the intergenerational social evil that prompts the monster/victim's return from the grave. When Samantha and David pay a visit to Grace, one of the victims in the 1969 case, they are told that 'nothing ever dies, it just changes form', that 'the children will suffer the sins of their fathers'. Indeed, Buck reveals his own father to be one of the high school boys involved in the Mary Banner disappearance, and it ultimately transpires that Samantha's stepfather, Bill, is Mary's boyfriend at the prom, and therefore Mary's killer.

Mary in ghost form resembles the wraiths of Japanese and Korean horror cinema, the vengeful female spirits who embody systematically repressed and invisible women of the past. Equally, *Candyman*'s influence on *Urban Legends: Bloody Mary* might be seen in Samantha's growing identification with Mary, reminiscent of Helen's affinity with the Candyman. 'Something's connecting me to what happened to these girls in 1969', Samantha muses early in the film, as she comes to realise that she is being haunted by the malefic spirit of Mary.

However, *Urban Legends: Bloody Mary* fails to follow through on these themes. It offers no commentary on date-rape culture. We never find out exactly what happened to Samantha and her friends when they were abducted by Buck and his buddies. (The police inform Samantha's parents that there are no signs of sexual abuse; however, Samantha herself later says to her friends, 'Who knows what they did to us after they locked us up? I sure as hell don't.') Likewise, 'the sins of the fathers' may be symbolically visited on Samantha and her friends when they are drugged and abducted like the girls in the '69 case, but the revelation that Samantha's stepfather, Bill, is a would-be rapist and murderer is presented merely as a clever plot-twist, and its broader implications go unexplored. Mary's victimisation is never fully visited upon Samantha; the wider issues of date-rape and sexual abuse are studiously avoided, and *Urban Legends: Bloody Mary* moves instead into a formulaic third act as Samantha sets out to find Mary's remains so she can bury them and lay Mary's soul to rest.

Urban Legends: Bloody Mary ultimately rejects meaningfulness for superficial action, reassuring banalities and a facile TV movie 'happy ending'. In the final coda, having achieved their goal (and defeated the evil stepfather in the process) Grace and Samantha realise in *Scooby-Doo* fashion that 'nobody will ever believe us'; that their ordeal will become 'just another ghost story'. The film ends on a hopelessly trite note as normality is restored and a television news reporter informs us that 'the decades-old mystery' of Mary's disappearance is finally solved.

BLOODY MARY (RICHARD VALENTINE, 2006)

At least two independently produced feature films (and a number of short films) have drawn on the Bloody Mary myth in their storylines. Richard Valentine's *Bloody Mary* (2006) relocates the legend to a state mental hospital in which a group of nurses ritually sacrifice one of their own to a wraith that inhabits the tunnels beneath the facility. The backstory informs us that in the 1970s a young woman named Mary was admitted to the institution obsessed with her own reflection. She was accosted by an orderly on whom she exacted bloody revenge by tearing out his eyes. Sedated from thereon she was never allowed near a mirror, until she escaped into the tunnels below the hospital where she starved to death. Thereafter Mary's legendary ghost is blamed for all the misfortunes that befall the hospital and its staff 'for everything from broken toilets to bad wiring'.

The nurses – led by Jenna (Danni Hamilton) – conspire to purge unbelievers from their circle by invoking Bloody Mary (which involves stripping naked in front of the mirror whilst reciting 'I believe in Bloody Mary'), who continues collecting the eyeballs of those who cross her. Little motivation is given to the nurses in playing the deadly mirror game, except for the vague explanation that 'the more you feed her, the longer she can stay on this side of the mirror'. This version of Bloody Mary, like the Candyman, seems to thrive on believers whilst systematically killing them off (thereby reducing her number of loyal followers drastically through the course of the film).

Director Valentine serves up atmosphere and mystery in place of logic, and plays on the idea of eisotrophobia (which, as the film's psychiatrist helpfully informs us, is an actual phobia based on the fear of mirrors). In this, *Bloody Mary* borrows liberally from the Mary Worth myth, which itself seems to derive in part from the phobia of mirrors and ghostly reflections in mirrors (the phobia is also known as spectrophobia and catoptrophobia), as well as from *Candyman, Hellraiser,* and a number of other eisotrophobia slashers/killers-trapped-in-mirrors horror movies such as *Mirrors* (2008) and *The Boogey Man* (1980).

THE LEGEND OF BLOODY MARY (JOHN STECENKO, 2008)

Lionsgate's 2008 straight-to-DVD release *The Legend of Bloody Mary* finds the legend's origins in the Salem witch trials (a popular variation of the Bloody Mary urban myth has the unfortunate Mary cast out as an eighteenth-century witch, rather than disfigured in a car-crash as per modern versions). In John Stecenko's film, the 16-year-old Mary Worth is found guilty of the sins of adultery and heresy, and sentenced to death at the stake; a large mirror is held up to her as she is physically mutilated. She vows revenge on her persecutors and begs the spirit of the mirror to take her. 'Now she's trapped in the mirror seeking vengeance, waiting for someone to believe in her and to release her,' we are informed, as the story moves to present day. 'Several poor souls wrote their names and those of their friends onto a mirror, and then believing in her, marked themselves for her vengeance.'

The poor souls in question are to include the nasty girl Jen (Brittany Miller) who, discovering the Bloody Mary curse on a website (www.Marked4Mary.com), decides to use it in a hazing ritual involving her friends. The girls subsequently end up dead, missing or in a mental hospital. Included in the ritual is Amy (Rachel Taylor) whose disappearance spurs her traumatised brother Ryan (Paul Preiss) to enlist the help of priest-cum-archaeologist, Father O'Neal (Robert J. Lock). Together they manage to track down the mirror trapping Mary's spirit, and by smashing it, are able to lift the curse.

Stecenko's intercutting of the three time periods, and the film's mishmash of influences, makes for a rather plodding, confused affair. *The Legend of Bloody Mary* steals liberally from *Candyman*, Arthur Miller's *The Crucible* and Japanese ghost stories. *The Exorcist* is another obvious inspiration, particularly in the make-up effects used to depict Bloody Mary and the inclusion of a priest-archaeologist à la Max von Sydow's Merrin. (Father O'Neal's attire throughout is in fact more befitting of Indiana Jones.)

Perhaps the most fascinating aspect of *The Legend of Bloody Mary* (despite making the Salem witch trials the 'allegorical moment', the film has little or nothing to say about the persecution of women) is the actual website featured in the film, created by Stecenko to promote the movie, and which includes an online game (Marked4Mary: The Game) offering prizes for disseminating and perpetuating the Bloody Mary legend: an ingenious (if morally dubious) form of digital 'ostension'.

BLOODY MARY POSSESSION (DARK LIBRA FILMS, 2016) & *BLOODY MARY* (DAVID HEAVENER, 2016)

More recently the Bloody Mary legend has inspired a number of new and emerging filmmakers, who have adapted the story to address contemporary concerns in their short films.

The ultra-low budget short, *Bloody Mary Possession* (2016) presents a recessionary narrative: twenty-something Mike (Cam Holmes) is severely depressed; stuck in a no-hope job, barely able to afford the mortgage on his clapboard house. To make matters worse, his girlfriend, Sam (Megan Lynn Losue) wants to get married and have children. In the laundry room Sam finds a mysterious message with instructions on how to play the Bloody Mary game, and the promise that her 'new friend' Mary will show her the future. Mike wakes next morning to find Sam under Mary's malefic influence and acting very strangely. Later, he discovers the black-haired skull of Bloody Mary and tries to flee the house, but is himself consumed by the wraith (in a welter of special effects).

Filmed in a bleak, snowy Libertyville, Illinois, *Bloody Mary Possession* turns the legend into a tale of economic precarity and despair in the younger generation. Mary's message to Mike and Sam is that the young people of today have no future – financially or otherwise.

The five minute short, *Bloody Mary* (2016), written by Drac von Stoller (a self-styled horror author based in Tennessee) offers a bare-bones retelling of the myth. At a dreary sixteenth birthday party, three friends decide to relieve their boredom playing the Bloody Mary game (it offers greater thrills than the alternative of watching *Paranormal Activity* on TV). They chant in front of the bathroom mirror and Bloody Mary (Lean Leonhardt) duly appears (looking suitably zombie-like) and plucks out their eyeballs. 'So, you think I'm stupid, huh?' Mary remonstrates. 'You don't believe in urban legends?' In stripping the legend to its barest essentials, *Bloody Mary* reaffirms it in the process.

Appendix: An Interview with Bernard Rose

The following interview between the author and Bernard Rose took place over lunch in West Hollywood on July 19, 2016.

You've said that a spiritual mentor would be Ken Russell, and I understand that you've also worked with Nicolas Roeg?

I've known Nic for a long time. Actually, I first met him through his son, Luc, who was producing music videos for me when I was doing music videos. Then Nic and I co-directed a film for Roger Waters, for a stage show that Roger did. We made a film that he projected and played in front of. Then I did a video for Roy Orbison that was a song from Nic's film *Insignificance* (1985), and it used parts of *Insignificance* in the video, so Nic was involved in that too. But I knew Nic socially for quite a while any way, and of course loved his work. I think the first film I saw of Nic's was *Don't Look Now* (1973), which is still to my mind one of the greatest horror films ever made. Up in the top three horror films – it's a perfect horror film. I learned a lot from Nic professionally. He had a background as a DP [Director of Photography], too. He very much approached the set from behind the camera, and I liked that. Ken did too, by the way. Ken always operated [a camera] on all of his films. He wasn't a DP in the way that Nic was – I mean Nic shot *Doctor Zhivago* (1965) – that's a DP! But, I mean, I don't think Ken ever lit a set but Nic clearly could.

You've talked about those directors following an alternative British cinema – an alternative to social realism.

Well, when I was a kid, there were three directors active in Britain who were my idols. There were Nic, Ken and [Stanley] Kubrick. Kubrick in the seventies was really a British director, essentially. I mean, *A Clockwork Orange* (1971) and *Barry Lyndon* (1975) – there's no other way of looking at them, really. They're Kubrick doing the two standard British genres – *A Clockwork Orange* is the social realist 'problem' picture, and *Barry Lyndon* is the costume drama – but his versions of both are so from a one hundred and eighty-degree perspective that you wouldn't even think of them as English films because they're enduring masterpieces, obviously. I think that Ken had the same thing going on.

Especially in the seventies, Ken made a string of masterpieces, really – *The Devils* (1971), *The Music Lovers* (1970), *Mahler* (1974), *Lisztomania* (1975).

And some of the BBC films?

Song of Summer (1968) is a masterpiece. And so is *The Debussy Film* (1965), and *Elgar* (1962) is incredible. He had a period from about '68 to… *Altered States* (1981) and *Crimes of Passion* (1984) when he still did really big films. They were so unique. In *Tommy* (1975), for example, Ken really invented the whole idea of the MTV clip. That came from *Tommy*, although it's been historically related back to Dick Lester. Dick Lester's film [*A Hard Day's Night*, 1964], when you actually look at it now, apart from the fact that it's actually about The Beatles, which gives it some appeal because the songs are very good, it's absolute garbage compared to *Tommy*. In *Tommy*, he treats the album like an opera, it's through song, there's not a title and not a word that's spoken in it, not one word, and you know everything that's going on the whole time. It's remarkable.

There's a real synthesis between the music and the image, isn't there?

And not only a synthesis, he's elaborating on the music: he's explaining the whole 1960s, he's saying the '60s is part of World War II, in a very graphic and direct way.

Something you've said about Ken Russell is that he follows in a Romantic tradition, like Powell and Pressburger.

The Devils is Ken's version of *Black Narcissus* (1947), you can argue that for sure. It comes from the same subject matter.

Do you also see parallels between Ken Russell and, say, Fellini, both of them starting out in Neorealism but ending up somewhere more flamboyant?

There are more parallels, I think, between Russell and Powell, than between Russell and Fellini. I think Fellini comes clearly out of the Italian neorealist tradition, and he developed from that towards fantasy, but even his most extreme fantasies like *Satyricon* (1969) are very factually based. So are Ken's, by the way, most of his films are biopics, even in *Lisztomania* everything that happens is factually true. But he's doing it in a Brechtian way. He's saying: I'm not going to pretend this isn't a pop star dressed as Franz Liszt.

When you were at film school, did you see yourself falling into any kind of tradition? Were you more drawn more towards one type of filmmaking than another?

I think I was before I went to film school, really. Although I have done things that are sort of realist, I never really… in the seventies in Britain, either you liked Ken Loach or Ken Russell, and I actually happen to like both of them, but for different reasons. I think sometimes people put people too much in pigeonholes. Loach's films are actually much more romantic than Ken Russell's. Ken is much more of a cynic than Loach. Loach believes the world is perfectible if only we all… you know…(laughs).

Do you see yourself combining elements of the two?

Sometimes I think you can. Neorealism is a style. People forget that. Loach had a very particular way of doing it that still feels current, if you look at *Kes* (1969), or something like that, you know? He is, of course, the other big British filmmaker from that era. The other that I really liked, who I think is often underrated now, is Lindsay Anderson, who I think combines those two traditions. He's like the mid-point between Loach and Russell, kind of.

He didn't make that many films, did he?

He made two masterpieces.

***O Lucky Man* (1973)?**

And *If…* (1968). *If…*, of course, is unquestionable. And there's a huge cross-fertilisation amongst those films [of that era]. I feel like *If…*, *A Clockwork Orange* and *O Lucky Man* are almost the same movie. If you run those three movies together, quite apart from the fact that they all star Michael McDowell, they tell you so much about England in that period.

That was really a great period for cinema in England. Even in the second tier you had people like Derek Jarman…

You started making films at quite a young age. Were you always a film enthusiast?

I was. I think I first got hold of an 8mm camera in the very early seventies, and was just playing with it. And I enjoyed that. I really enjoyed the action of making films. And of course in that era it was making a silent film, really.

Did the camera come to you through your family?

No, I got a hold of one. Initially, I borrowed somebody's, I think. But then I got one because I wanted it. And then pretty soon I graduated to a clockwork Bolex, at the age of thirteen. I think I used my Bar Mitzvah money to buy a Bolex.

So you were already working on 16mm as a teenager?

I was working on 16mm reversal stock, and I think people forget now that it was a very difficult stock to use: it had a latitude of about one and a half stops, so if the exposure was incorrect, either it would be white or it would be black. So it was really hard to get an image.

Was that the old news-film stock?

It wasn't news film, it was 25 ASA Kodachrome. It was beautiful stuff. It never fades. It was indestructible, actually. It had very, very saturated colours; that was its unique quality, but it was staggeringly slow – 25 ASA outdoors, daylight! On a dull day you couldn't get an exposure, it was that bad.

Did you have lights?

I did eventually get lights, because to actually shoot at all indoors you had to have quite powerful lights; I remember buying a 2K light because if you didn't have it you weren't going to shoot anything. So I suppose, yes, for a teenager it was quite sophisticated what I had, you see, because I acquired the stuff.

What kinds of films were you making back then? Were they pastiches of movies you liked?

No, in fact, they weren't. In 1975, the BBC used to have a competition for best amateur film. I don't know if you remember the show?

With Michael Rodd?

No, it was John Craven. It was a show made out of BBC Manchester; I remember going to the studio because I won the competition with a film that was about a terrorist blowing up a restaurant in Tottenham Court Road. Quite ambitious for a teenager. I remember sending it into the BBC. It was 16mm and it had sound on it – not dialogue, but it had music and sound effects, which I had mixed and put on the stripe. And I sent it into the BBC and I remember them calling me the next day. The producer called my house, and kind of grilled me about it for a long time because he didn't think I'd made the film without adult supervision. I think the real reason he thought that was because the cast of the film were all adults. In fact the guy said to me that out of all the submissions they'd ever had, I was the only person who'd submitted a film with adult actors in it. And I was like, it's supposed to be a terrorist, I can't cast a child! To me this seemed an absurdity, that I would cast a child to play somebody like that.

So it was the professionalism of the film that won the award for you? Its ambition?

I think they were a little taken aback by it. But I'd been doing it for quite a while by then and had gotten quite sophisticated at it.

How many films did you make before going to the National Film and Television School?

Quite a few. I would say, ten or fifteen. A lot. And they got more ambitious during the seventies. And then after I won the competition, I had a friend who worked for Samuelsons, which was the big rental house in Cricklewood. And we used to load up gear on a Friday night that wasn't being rented – and take it! And so after 1976/1977 I started making films using an Éclair NPR and other sophisticated, synchronous 16mm cameras and Nagra tape recorders. So then I could record dialogue and I started shooting black and white negative. So the films I was making looked professional, even though nobody was paying for them, by the way. I was stealing equipment and just making them with whatever I could.

Were you functioning as your own DP at that stage?

Absolutely, yes, I was shooting them all.

Which you came back to doing more recently [since *Ivansxtc*].

That's right. I think that's what gave me the confidence, thinking: it can't be any harder than using 25 ASA Kodachrome. Anything digital is just so easy to use. I mean, now, of course, iPhones shoot 4K, so you literally can do a movie on your phone now.

Why did you pick the NFTS, why not another school like the Royal College of Art? What was it about that school that attracted you?

Before I went to film school I was working for Jim Henson on *The Muppet Show* and on *The Dark Crystal* (1982), and we were working out at Elstree Studios, so I had some professional experience by then. I remember when we were doing *The Dark Crystal*, at the time they were just finishing *The Shining* (1980), and the set of the hotel was still in the backlot, the exterior and the maze part of it, and they were shooting *Raiders of the Lost Ark* (1981) in the studio, and Warren Beatty was doing *Reds* (1981). So it was like the last burst of the great seventies period of Elstree. Kubrick, Spielberg, Jack Nicholson, it was pretty starry!

How did that professional experience lead to the NFTS?

I just literally applied to them. I didn't have a degree, because I'd worked for Jim. But I had films that I'd made and I had professional experience. At the time the film school was run by a man called Colin Young, who was very against the idea of it being an academic place, and very much wanted it to be a practical, vocational school. And he wanted to encourage people to be filmmakers. I don't think he was that interested in making people competent professionals. He'd had a lot of success at UCLA, taught Coppola and I think Jim Morrison was a student of his. He definitely had this sort of loose approach; he wanted people who were good, more than anything. That was the thing: you had to show what you could do.

Where did you used to see movies when you were a teenager? On TV?

No, not really. None of these movies were on television. They were all in the theatres. I don't know if *The Devils* has ever been on television.

Was there a movie house that you'd go to regularly? Like a rep cinema?

Oh, yes, absolutely. I lived in north London. So I used to go to a whole bunch of them.

The Everyman in Hampstead…

The Phoenix in Finchley?

…The Phoenix. In Hendon, there was the Classic. There was The Screen on the Hill, of course. The one in Islington…

Screen on the Green…

There were a lot of movie theatres. And, of course, The Scala. I actually worked in some of those theatres. I worked in the Screen on the Hill on Hampstead Hill for a while.

How did you support yourself through film school?

In that era, not only was it free but they gave you a grant. *And* they gave you money to buy 16mm film, I mean, they wouldn't do that now. They used to give us a stipend. But, anyway, prior to working on The Muppets I worked in movie theatres, and it was true that if you worked in the independent theatres in London, we used to let the staff from the other movie theatres in for free, and they used to let us in for free. Basically you could go to see anything without paying.

Was the move into music videos a pragmatic choice – a need to find employment after film school?

Not really, no.

Were you drawn to it aesthetically, because of your interest in music?

I was, yes.

Because it was very new then, wasn't it?

Very new. I remember the first one I made, no-one even knew what it was. They were like, *what* are you doing? You're going to make a *what*? I was still at film school when I started doing them. I was still a student when I did the first one, which was, luckily for me, 'Red Red Wine', a UB40 record, which was a hit all over the world – which never hurts.

You made a video album for them, *Labour of Love*?

Basically what happened was, I met with the sax player from the band, Brian Travers, and he had this idea to hire a film school student who would be cheaper. He was going to run the show, I think, and it was his idea.

Did you look towards *Tommy* as inspiration?

I did. Absolutely. I mean not consciously, but I think definitely. So Brian and I did that first one and the record was so successful and the video was successful. So then he said, why don't we expand it into the whole album, and I said, absolutely, let's do it. Like I said, I was still at the film school and I had to make a graduation film, so I said, I'll do it and just make it my graduation film. So that's what *Labour of Love* was originally. People were saying, you're crazy, you want to make a musical? And whilst I was making it, they were saying, what's this nonsense, you're making a musical? And, of course, by the time it was finished, it was a musical with international hit records, which is a very different thing, isn't it? (laughs)

And suddenly everybody was making music videos. Do you agree, though, that it's a form that never really fulfilled its potential?

Well, when we were doing it, in the early '80s, like I said, in that instance UB40 were on their own independent label – they used to distribute through Virgin – and so they then had complete control over what they did. And we did things that were considered unacceptable at the time, like shooting it in black and white, like letterboxing it. I remember when it was first done the BBC rejected it on quality control grounds, because they said with the letterboxing and black and white they couldn't show it. But the record went to number one and it went to number one very quickly, and they had no studio band for *Top of the Pops*, so they were forced to show it. But it was absolutely against their will. And, of course, after that everybody's video was letterboxed in black and white. It's funny how that was considered radical then, but it was. The BBC tech guys were concerned that people would think their TVs had gone wrong.

It was using a movie convention.

It was, and people understood that right away, but it failed Q.C., I remember that. Anyway, I think there was a lot of potential but what happened is what always happens – it became a big business, and then people realised that they needed to have a music video department at the record company, so suddenly there was somebody you had to report to who was going to vet the ideas. Certainly when I made the Frankie Goes to Hollywood stuff, I made that and I delivered it to them, and they'd shake their heads and go, we can't show this, what is this nonsense? That was a lucky thing that happened, of course, the scandal [of 'Relax'], that record was huge, but there were other ones we did and they just never showed the videos. Now obviously they started to say, ah, and censorship came in. It's gone now. Now on YouTube you can have a video that has anything happen in it. I think it's changed. Now corporate video has a different function. In a way it's more important now. I don't think it's gone away.

Artistically?

It depends. Sometimes there are people, like Kanye West, who does videos that can have an impact. I think it's still there with the right record and the right artist doing the right thing. All the videos I did in the '80s, every single one of them is on YouTube, every single one of them. So in a weird way they are much more available now than they were then.

You never went back to music videos though?

The last one I did was for Roy Orbison.

Why have you not gone back?

A number of reasons… too busy, and music videos is very much a young man's game, you know. I was 23 when I started doing them. I would do it again for the right record. Nobody asks me!

All your films seem to take a delight in rethinking the format. *Ivansxtc*, especially, seemed to be a big turning point in your career in that respect.

Well, the technology had certainly changed, in a way now that's hard not to regret (laughs). But, it was inevitable, I think. When I first saw those cameras, I thought, this is it, this is all over, it's finished. And it is now, for sure. But now you have the opposite problem – too many people are making movies who shouldn't be. Just because you can doesn't mean you should.

But aren't there still the gatekeepers in terms of distribution?

I think the gatekeepers have gotten worse, because they can't filter the volume of stuff. So now distribution has become narrower and narrower, and harder and harder to penetrate -just generally from the noise of how much stuff there is out there. Never mind videos, talking about photographs, I was reading a statistic – this was about four years ago – they'd reached a point where, on any given day, as many photos were taken as were taken in the entire history of photography up to that moment.

And they're not being archived…

The sheer volume of image taking has so increased, which is why we see shots of things we never used to see before, all the time. And video – we're all carrying 4K cameras in our pocket. That's a social and artistic change in the world, so why is your video going to be so much more interesting than anybody else's? I think the flip side to that is we've all got the technology to write *War and Peace*, but we're not all Tolstoy, you know?

But I would argue that somebody like you has the skill and the talent, and the sheer ability to put something together on a low budget that works, and that has the production value and the narrative know-how.

Actually, production value's absolutely meaningless. What matters is whether the film's powerful enough.

Production value in the sense that, for example, *Frankenstein* is a movie set in modern times and all the locations are right for it. In the same way that *Candyman*, although a low budget, had locations that were right for that film. That comes down to skill and expertise, not necessarily money. That's what I mean by production values, that they are right for the project.

That's right, yes. You deal with whatever the technology of the day is. And also what the financial structure of the day is, because, as I say, it's changing. The problem now is all to do with distribution. I think, unquestionably, there's been a narrative about the cinema of the '70s that's become accepted through books like *Easy Riders, Raging Bulls*. I think it's a really pernicious piece of shit, that book.

Because it suggests that the directors were all coked up and everything was done on the fly?

Implying that all the executives weren't! Who do you think they were partying with? It's absolute garbage. It has about as much meaning as saying Modigliani drank too much. Maybe that's a problem if you're meeting him at 12.30 on a Friday night and he's incoherent, but what's that got to do with anything in terms of his work and the quality of it? I think it's a very moralistic point of view and disguises the true agenda, which is, by the early '80s, the government – I don't just mean the US government, but *all* governments – had lost control of what they considered a critical propaganda tool. The most obvious and extreme example of that was *Apocalypse Now* (1979), where the filmmaker, using his own money, which they'd given to him previously, and made damn sure that wouldn't happen again, had gone off and made not this little independent film about Vietnam, but this giant, epic, huge, monumental film about Vietnam, the one you came out of no-one was left in any doubt – not intellectually but viscerally – that the US had lost the Vietnam war. And somebody said: this has got to stop. You've lost control. This guy is telling everybody we lost that war. Not telling you in a prettied way, but in a way that you will never forget. Like by having the Playboy Bunnies helicoptered out. That scene tells you every single thing you will ever need to know, and the image is directly reflecting the image of the helicopter leaving the embassy in Saigon… it's incredible, staggering filmmaking. And it's very political in a way that's way beyond anything you see nowadays.

Does that go hand-in-hand with the end of independence in Hollywood in the eighties?

I think the point is that they said 'that's got to stop', and within seven years they were making *Top Gun* (1986). They took control between those years. And the way they did it was to say, this Michael Cimino, he's out of control. Again, you look at the content. What is the subject matter of *Heaven's Gate* (1980)? 'The federal government is going to come in and murder you.' Don't imagine that their dislike of that film doesn't have something to do with its content.

A similar thing happened in the thirties with the Production Code, as a way to take back control of distribution from the state censors.

That happened as a result of the Fatty Arbuckle scandal. That was more about survival. And that was more of a reaction against the extreme pressure groups. I actually think that the studios taking over the reins creatively in the '80s was run by the MPAA, was run by Jack Valenti specifically, and filmmaking did change in that period, when suddenly people who'd been embraced were suspects, and it was as much a closing down of subject matter as it was budgets. Because it's not like these filmmakers stopped working. But suddenly Coppola's making *Peggy Sue Got Married* (1986) instead of *Apocalypse Now*.

Is that what happened to you with *Ivansxtc*? It wasn't about the budget, it was about the subject matter?

It was about two things – and it wasn't even about the subject matter, it was about something else. It was about the fact that I could make that film without their knowledge, or their approval. And if I made money with it, they were dead. So they had to make sure that I wouldn't make any money with it. And they have to make sure that nobody can make money with independent films that people self-produce, because if somebody does, what use do they have for an agent? If you could spend thirty thousand dollars and sell a film for a million, who wants an agent? Without your fee at that point, that's a straight profit business. But they make damn sure you can't do that. You can try to do that, but it's a bit like trying to open a restaurant in a street with a bunch of mafia bosses. They just won't let you. They just won't. You can pretend the world isn't that way but it *is* that way.

Is it just the agents? Or is it also the studios afraid of not getting their overheads?

The agents are just the interface, just the lowly foot soldiers. No, it's a huge power structure that goes all the way to the very top. And it has very specific reasons and aims.

So what you did was in effect say, you know what, we can make films and they don't have to cost that amount of money, and that was what they didn't like because –

It meant they couldn't get paid.

Is it still the same?

It's worse. That's what I'm saying. Now you absolutely can't make money doing a film like that. Before, you might have if you had a fluke chance and somehow you cut in the right person who ushered you into the right door. But now, forget it. It's not happening. It doesn't matter what your film is, what it's about, how good it is, or even who's in it. No. That's it. No. But, of course, they won't say, because it's like a dam behind a giant reservoir. Eventually it's going to explode and they'll have no control over it. This isn't just to do with movies, this is something that's happening in the world now. The whole tech world is about charging you for things that used to be for free. Uber is my favourite example. I remember I went to Russia in the '90s to make *Anna Karenina*. I was there a long time, long enough to no longer be staying in a hotel, long enough to learn how to act like a native, and I remember the public transport doesn't work after midnight in St Petersburg, and people are always out until three or four in the morning. So how do people get home? There were no taxis. The only taxis were those that hung around the hotel, whose job was to overcharge tourists and carry contraband. So how do most people get around in Russia, and – actually to this day – they would just stand on the street corner and put their hand up. And any car – whoever it was – would pull over. They'd tell the driver where they wanted to go. The driver would tell them how much it's going to cost them. They'd jump in. And that's how transportation works in Russia. That's Uber! But nobody's taking a cut of it. So now they tell us, you can't do that because you're at risk – you don't know whose car you're getting in. I used to talk to these young girls going home drunk, and say to them: isn't this dangerous? And they'd be like, no, if we don't like the look of the guy we don't get in the car.

I've even seen that in American TV dramas – 'If you get in a cab make sure it's an Uber!'

It's neither more safe nor more dangerous! Just because the guy's got a light on his car he's neither a killer nor a rapist? I mean, what nonsense!

It's just another form of regulation.

It's just a way for them to get a cut. So now we have this thing called the internet. Now all the money goes to Facebook or Google, or whatever. Not to the content providers whose copyrights are basically violated flagrantly. Sooner or later there's going to be a class action. Sooner or later the internet service providers have to understand that they have to pay for what they're supplying to people. Sooner or later none of it will matter because the whole revenue system will just be on clicks online. There won't be any money anymore. There'll be some version of Bitcoin. You won't see any money, it'll just be some fantasy. So I think that obviously there's some huge power shift because of that and movies are certainly affected.

Distribution is always going to be very difficult to control, isn't it?

Trying to maintain a monopoly in the face of the torrent of the internet is so hard it's unbearable. The only place they can have any success is gap-fill exhibition. Obviously there are only 52 weeks in a year, there are never going to be 53. So, really, the movies are a Friday to Monday business. Mid-week revenues are negligible and always have been. So some weekends aren't very good box office, such as Halloween, which is actually a very bad weekend, everyone's at parties; Superbowl and other events which we can't compete with. So there are only, say, 38 weekends that are really prime for the movies. So if studios release one film each on those weekends they cannibalise themselves. The box office is only so big. If they release twice as many films, their expenses more than double and the same amount of money comes back. Obviously, it makes so much more sense for them to release fewer films, take more of the money and increase their margins. The only way they can possibly do that is by inflating budgets. And the only way you can really inflate a budget now is to basically make animated films. Most of these films are essentially animated, most of them are shot against green screen, all the superhero films.

So using virtual sets doesn't actually save money, it inflates budgets?

Yes, because it's a way to make the costs impossible for anybody to actually account. Because then they're outsourcing all the CGI work to wherever, it doesn't matter where. They can say the film cost whatever they say it cost.

No auditing?

They can try! But that's always been the case. I mean, the whole idea that these films cost two hundred million dollars is hilarious. It's not true. They don't have two hundred million dollars of expenses. And also a lot of the time they're taking the money out of one pocket and putting it in the other, like ABC is owned by Disney, so when a Disney is advertised on ABC, spending twenty million dollars on advertising, they're just taking it out of one pocket and putting it in the other.

Let's talk a little bit about the horror genre. One word Clive Barker has used, and that you've used, in relation to the genre is transgression. Horror is a transgressive genre that revolves around taboo subject matter – certainly the horror films that you've made, *Snuff-Movie*, for example; and *Frankenstein*'s always been a taboo because of the idea of creating a human from the dead. Where would you want to take the genre from here? If you had carte blanche?

Nowadays making a film is a bit like working in the Soviet era in Russia, where anything that you actually want to say has to be codified to such an extent that the party censors can't spot what it is. Because films are on television, and television is basically a branch of advertising. Television is only ever about selling products, and they don't want the look and the feel of the film to be too much different to the commercials, because they don't want it to stick out too much, they want you to stay watching the commercials. And they're funded by advertising, all the front-line stuff is all funded by advertising. So the primary concern is keeping the manufacturers and advertisers happy; but if you want to transgress, if you want to have a horror film, you want to frighten people. That's why mainstream horror has become exclusively about jump scares. Just coming up behind someone and saying "boo" is not very transgressive. If you look at the works of someone like Tod Browning, or [David] Cronenberg, it's transgressive, because it's about things which are upsetting, and that's what horror should be. I think, for me, the whole point about the horror genre is that people regard it as trash so they don't take any notice of it. And it's true of course that most horror films are not very ambitious. They're just about killing teenagers or whatever. And I think that if ninety percent or ninety-nine percent of them are trash, the one percent that aren't trash are the best films ever made. And have been made by the best directors, everybody from Kubrick to [Roman] Polanski to Ken Russell to Ingmar Bergman to Lars von Trier. The most cinematic directors choose horror because it's a visceral medium. And if you can disturb someone… Pasolini – I would regard *Salo* (1975) as a horror film. How else could you describe it? Certainly, *The Devils* is a horror film.

And, as you say, Bergman.

Hour of the Wolf (1968). Actually, *Fanny and Alexander* (1982) has the structure of a horror film, and it's very frightening. The whole thing with the evil bishop and the ghosts, very scary. *Fanny and Alexander* was a huge influence on *Paperhouse*. It had that really effective creepy feel to it, dreamlike, nightmarish feel.

Candyman revolves around that doesn't it? Really nothing happens for the first forty-five minutes. It's all about the *idea* of dread, and the build-up of dread.

In fact, when you look at *Halloween* – the original John Carpenter film – it's just about people walking around a suburban setting. Really nothing happens for almost the whole movie. It's brilliant. It's just pure suspense.

You've said something interesting about *Candyman*. That you thought the second half was maybe not as successful as the first half. In the sense that maybe the second half does necessarily use some of the more conventional tropes of the horror genre, like: is she going insane, is she not going insane?

It is and it isn't. I think it's difficult to say now in retrospect because in the second half of the film you get Tony Todd's performance which is wonderful, and he adds so much to the whole thing. But, yes, once you bring on the monster, it's always a bit like… there's a lessening of the dread, I suppose. I mean, the film does change, and as you say, it becomes about whether or not she's insane.

It reminded me a little of some of the 1940s films, where you had this whole cycle of movies about paranoid women –

Like *Gaslight*?

– Is she being driven insane deliberately? *Gaslight*, yes.

There's a Hitchcock film, what's it called? With Cary Grant.

Suspicion. That was another film that came to mind. My last question then, is how much was Hitchcock an influence in terms of the filmmaking grammar? When I watched *Candyman* again recently, it reminded me very much of what Hitchcock said about subjective cinema. For example, there's a sequence where

Virginia Madsen's alone in her apartment, and goes down this long corridor, and you see her point of view. You get the reverse shot of the mirror at the end of the corridor, the bathroom cabinet, then you get the shot of her as she looks to see if there's somebody in the kitchen. I got the idea that might have been the way Hitchcock would have shot that sequence.

I think it's more the way Polanski would have shot it. I think for me the biggest influences on the film were Polanski, for sure, certainly *The Tenant* (1976) and *Rosemary's Baby* (1968) which are pillars of the genre. And *Repulsion* (1965) as well, I guess. And they're all about women alone in an apartment, I mean, you were talking about that sequence – I think it has more parallels to *Repulsion* than in anything Hitchcock did. But there is also a very clear difference between the way Polanski would shoot a scene like that and Hitchcock. Hitchcock does exactly what you're describing: shot/reaction shot. If you actually go back and look at the scene in *Candyman*, that's not how it's cut. The camera follows her and moves with her, which is –

More Polanski.

Yeah, and more what Kubrick would do actually, in *The Shining*. I would say the big influences on the film were *The Exorcist* – I'm thinking of the films I was looking at a lot before I did it – and *Fanny and Alexander*. The way that Bergman creates dread is very interesting. He always makes things go very quiet. It's a very good trick. If things are quiet you immediately tense up in a horror film. Keep the score banging on the whole time, you kind of get bored!

WORKS CITED

Abbott, S. (2015) 'Candyman and Saw: Reimagining the Slasher Film through Urban Gothic', in Clayton, W. (ed.) *Style and Form in the Hollywood Slasher Film*. Basingstoke: Palgrave Macmillan, pp. 67–78.

Balasopoulos, A. (1997) 'The demon of (racial) history: Reading Candyman.' *Gramma: Journal of Theory and Criticism*, 5, pp. 25–47.

Barker, C. (1985) 'The Forbidden'. *Clive Barker's Books of Blood: Vol.5*. London: Sphere.

Benshoff, H. (2000) 'Blaxploitation Horror Films: Generic Reappropriation of Reinscription.' *Cinema Journal*, 39, pp. 31-50.

Blouin, M.J. (2016) 'Candyman and Neoliberal Racism', in *Magical Thinking, Fantastic Film, and the Illusions of Neoliberalism*. New York: Palgrave Macmillan, pp. 81–108.

Briefel, A. and Ngai, S. (1996) '"How much did you pay for this place?" Fear, entitlement, and urban space in Bernard Rose's Candyman.' *Camera Obscura: Feminism, Culture, and Media Studies*, 13(1 37), pp. 69–91.

Briefel, A. and Ngai, S. (2000) 'Candyman: urban space, fear, and entitlement', in Silver, A. and Ursini, J. (eds.) *The Horror Film Reader*. New York: Limelight Editions, pp. 281–304.

Brunvand, J. H. (1981) *The Vanishing Hitchhiker: American Urban Legends and their Meanings*. New York: W.W. Norton & Co.

Cowan, N. (1992) 'The Fabulist of Terror.' *Eye*, pp. 17-19.

Church, D. (2006) 'Return of the Return of the Repressed: Notes on the American Horror Film (1991-2006).' *Offscreen, vol.10, issue 10*. Available at: http://offscreen.com/view/return_of_the_repressed (Accessed: 1 October 2016).

Condon, B. (1995) *Candyman: Farewell to the Flesh*.

Cooper, P. (2014) 'Tony Todd Talks 'Candyman', Filming In the Projects, and His Legacy'. *Bloody Disgusting*. Available at: http://bloody-disgusting.com/interviews/3319027/interview-tony-todd-talks-candyman-filming-projects-legacy/ (Accessed: 19 February 2017).

Christensen, D. (2001) 'Candyman'. Available at: http://philipglass.com/films/candyman/ (Accessed: 18 February 2017).

Christensen, D. (2001b) 'Notes on the Music of Candyman.' Available at: http://philipglass.com/recordings/candyman_music_of/ (Accessed: 18 February 2017).

Creed, B. (1986) 'Horror and the monstrous-feminine: An imaginary abjection', *Screen*, 27(1), pp. 44–71. Reprinted in Jancovich, M. (ed.) *The Horror Film Reader*. London: Routledge, 2002, pp. 67-76.

Donaldson, L.F. (2011) 'The suffering black male body and the threatened white female body': Ambiguous bodies in Candyman.' *The Irish Journal of Gothic and Horror Studies, 9*. Available at: http://irishgothichorrorjournal.homestead.com/Candyman.html (Accessed: 28 September 2016).

Ebert, R. (1992) 'Candyman.' *Chicago-Sun Times*. Available at: http://www.rogerebert.com/reviews/candyman-1992 (Accessed: 19 February 2017).

Emery, D. (2016) 'Bloody Mary in the Mirror: The Urban Legend'. *ThoughtCo*. Available at http://www.thoughtco.com/bloody-mary-in-the-mirror-3299478 (Accessed: 21 February 2017).

French, T. (1995) 'Candyman 2.' *Cinefantastique*. Vol 26, No. 3 (April), pp. 8-10.

Grant, B.K. (2015) 'Introduction' in Grant (ed.) *The Dread of Difference: Gender and the Horror Film*. Second edn. Austin: University of Texas Press, pp.1-16.

Green, T. (1992) 'Barker, More than Just a "Hellraiser."' *USA Today*. 24 September.

Hester-Williams, K.D. (2004) 'NeoSlaves: Slavery, Freedom, and African American Apotheosis in Candyman, The Matrix and The Green Mile'. *Genders, Vol 40*. Available at: https://www.atria.nl/ezines/IAV_606661/IAV_606661_2011_53/genders/g40_williams.html (Accessed: 29 September 2016).

Hill, M. (1997) 'Can Whiteness Speak? Institutional Anomies, Ontological Disasters, and Three Hollywood Films', in Wray, M. and Newitz, A. (eds.) *White Trash: Race and Class in America*. New York: Routledge, pp. 155–157.

Hoeveler, D.L. (2007) 'The postfeminist filmic female gothic detective: reading the bodily text in Candyman.', in Brabon, B.A. and Genz, S. (eds) *Postfeminist Gothic: Critical Interventions in Contemporary Culture*. Basingstoke: Palgrave Macmillan, pp. 99–113.

Hutchings, P. (2004) *The Horror Film*. Harlow, Essex: Pearson Educational.

Jackson, K. (1993) 'The Sweet Smell of Excess'. *The Independent*. Available at: http://www.independent.co.uk/arts-entertainment/interview-the-sweet-smell-of-excess-bernard-rose-has-an-oral-fixation-kevin-jackson-talked-to-him-1497390.html (Accessed: 30 September 2016).

Jancovich, M. (2007) 'Crack-Up: Psychological Realism, Generic Transformation and the Demise of the Paranoid Woman's Film.' *The Irish Journal of Gothic and Horror Studies, 3*. Available at: https://irishgothichorror.wordpress.com/issue3/ (Accessed: 14 April 2017).

Kee, J.B. (2015) 'Black Masculinities and Postmodern Horror: Race, Gender, and Abjection.' *Visual Culture & Gender, 10*. Available at: http://vcg.emitto.net/ (Accessed 12 December 16).

Koven, M.J. (1999) 'Candyman Can: Film and Ostension'. *Contemporary Legend, 2*, pp. 155-173.

Kuhn, A. (2000) '"What's the matter, Trevor? Scared of something?": Representing the Monstrous-feminine in Candyman'. *Erfurt Electronic Studies in English*. Available at: http://webdoc.sub.gwdg.de/edoc/ia/eese/artic20/kuhn/kuhn.html (Accessed: 28 September 2016).

Landekic, L. (2016) 'Candyman.' *Art of the Title*. Available at: http://www.artofthetitle.com/title/candyman/ (Accessed: 19 February 2017).

Lovell, G. (1992) 'Black slasher "Candyman" draws fire over "racist" depictions.' *The Chicago Tribune*. Available at: http://articles.chicagotribune.com/1992-10-29/features/9204080203_1_candyman-white-women-tony-todd (Accessed: 30 September 2016).

McDonagh, M. (1995) 'A Kind of Magic.' *The Dark Side*, 45 (April/May), pp. 22-27.

Maslin, J. (1992) 'Candyman: Science-Fiction Horrors in a Housing Project.' *The New York Times*. Available at: http://www.nytimes.com/movie/review?res=9E0CE2DF123EF935A25 753C1A964958260 (Accessed: 19 February 2017).

Means Coleman, R. R. (2011) 'Black is Back! Retribution and the Urban Terrain: 1990s', in *Horror Noire: Blacks in American Horror Films from the 1890s to Present*. New York: Routledge, pp. 169-197.

Meyer, T. (1999) *Candyman: Day of the Dead*.

Pinedo, I.C. (1997) 'Race Horror', in *Recreational Terror: Women and the Pleasures of Horror Film Viewing*. Albany: State University of New York Press, pp. 111–132.

Rose, B. (1991) *Candyman*. Screenplay. Draft Revised (August 1991).

Rose, B. (1992) *Candyman*.

Schwarz, J. (2004a) *Clive Barker: Raising Hell*.

Schwarz, J. (2004b) *Sweets to the Sweet: The Candyman Mythos*.

Schweiger, D. (1992) 'Bernard Rose's Demons of the Mind.' *Fangoria*, 118, pp. 12-18.

Sharrett, C. (1993) 'The horror film in neoconservative culture', *Journal of Popular Film and Television*, 21(3), pp. 100–110. Reprinted in Grant, B.K. (ed.) *The Dread of Difference: Gender and the Horror Film*. Austin: University of Texas Press, Second edn., 2015. pp. 281-304.

Snyder, L.A. (2009) 'Art and the Artist: An Interview with Clive Barker.' *Strange Horizons*. Available at: http://strangehorizons.com/non-fiction/articles/art-and-the-artist-an-interview-with-clive-barker/ (Accessed: 19 February 2017).

Thomas, K. (1992) 'Ambitious "Candyman" Serves Large Doses of Repellent Gore.' *Los Angeles Times*. Available at: http://articles.latimes.com/1992-10-16/entertainment/ca-39_1_bernard-rose (Accessed: 19 February 2017).

Thompson, K.M. (2007) 'Strange Fruit: Candyman and Supernatural Dread', in *Apocalyptic Dread: American Film at the Turn of the Millennium*. Albany: State University of New York Press.

Variety (1991). Candyman. Available at http://variety.com/1991/film/reviews/candyman-2-1200429445/ (Accessed: 18 February 2017).

Wells, P. (2002) 'On the Side of the Demons: Clive Barker's Pleasures and Pains', in Chibnall, S. and Petley, J. (eds) *British Horror Cinema*. London: Routledge, pp. 172–182.

Williams, L. (1983) 'When the Woman Looks', in Doane, M.A, Mellancamp, P., and Williams, L. (eds.) *Re-vision: Essays in Feminist Film Criticism*, Frederick, Md: University Publications/American Film Institute. Reprinted in Jancovich, M. (ed.) *The Horror Film Reader*. London: Routledge, 2002 pp. 61–66.

Williams, L. (2001) *When Women Look: A Sequel. Senses of Cinema*. Available at: http://sensesofcinema.com/2001/freuds-worst-nightmares-psychoanalysis-and-the-horror-film/horror_women/ (Accessed: 19 December 2016).

Williams, T. (2015) 'Trying to Survive on the Darker Side: 1980s Family Horror', in Grant, B.K. (ed.) *The Dread of Difference: Gender and the Horror Film*. Austin: University of Texas Press, pp. 192–208.

Wood, R. (2003) *Hollywood from Vietnam to Reagan…and Beyond*. New York: Columbia University Press.

Wyrick, L. (1998) 'Summoning Candyman: The cultural production of history', *Arizona Quarterly: A Journal of American Literature, Culture, and Theory*, 54(3), pp. 89–117.

DEVIL'S ADVOCATES

"Auteur Publishing's new Devil's Advocates critiques on individual titles offer bracingly fresh perspectives from passionate writers. The series will perfectly complement the BFI archive volumes." Christopher Fowler, Independent on Sunday

CARRIE – NEIL MITCHELL

"Top notch... intelligent... insightful." – Total Film

"... [goes] into exhaustive detail on the genesis of the film... a brisk, enjoyable read. *****" – Frightfest.co.uk

HALLOWEEN – MURRAY LEEDER

"Murray Leeder's thoughtful, clearly expressed analysis is far reaching in scope while resisting the temptation to become sidetracked... a joy to read; it's insightful and well researched and serves as an encouragement to return to Halloween once again" – Exquisite Terror

SUSPIRIA – ALEXANDRA HELLER-NICHOLAS

"... at once original and deeply subversive... This is a really sharp book, and an excellent series... Brief, compact, and authoritative, these are the volumes to beat on these classic genre films." – Wheeler Winston Dixon

THE TEXAS CHAIN SAW MASSACRE – JAMES ROSE

"[James Rose] find[s] new and unusual perspectives with which to address [the] censor-baiting material. Unsurprisingly, the effect... is to send the reader back to the films... watch the films, read these Devil's Advocates analyses of them." – Crime Time